A Watchman Over Christ's Church

by C. Matthew McMahon

Copyright Information

A Watchman Over Christ's Church by C. Matthew McMahon
Edited by Therese B. McMahon

Table of Contents

Introduction

If you are a minister of the Gospel, are you a *faithful* watchman for the Lord? Have you ever been called *a watchman?* In one of the most significant ministerial books of the 19th century, Alexander Vinet said, "The minister's life is a life of consecration, without which it has no meaning."[1] The importance of the statement is lost without understanding what a minister of the Gospel, or *watchman for the Lord,* actually is. Such marks and qualifications of the office of *watchman* under Jesus Christ for the good of his church, demonstrate a man's capacity to leads others in the Christian life, having spiritual maturity as one who also continually leads his own family in the spiritual disciplines, and grows and conforms to the image of Jesus Christ day to day. He is consecrated to God, and his house is a little church.[2] Whatever his private piety is, and whatever his home life is, is what is brought into

---

[1] Vinet, Alexander, *Pastoral Theology or the Theory of the Evangelical Ministry,* (Crossville, TN: Puritan Publications, 2017) 46.

[2] How can a minister successfully minister to others? "To observe the order of St. Paul (Acts 20:28; 1 Tim. 4:16), a minister must begin with himself, fulfill his own duties, and care for his own salvation before all things. Before going abroad from love to his neighbor, let him withdraw into the secret place of the divine holiness. Before compassionating the misery of others, let him be sensible of his own ills and of his own weaknesses. And, before urging others to obey the law of God, let him first obey it himself. The first duty of a bishop is to be holy." Duguet, Jacqeus Joseph, *Traite des Devoirs d'un Eveque,* art. ii., § 1.

the church, for good or for ill. He is to be consecrated to God, and so, he seeks to make converts to his way of life, which is in fact, Christ's way of life.

Personal piety is absolutely indispensable for the success of a watchman outside his closet.[3] Thomas Murphy says, "It is beyond all question that this eminent piety is before everything else in preparation for the duties of the sacred office."[4] This is where the minister first assesses how he may maintain and advance the highest degree of holiness in his personal walk, before he takes on advancing holiness in the life of the congregation through his duties.[5]

The church of Jesus Christ is the place God has chosen to reveal his divine character. To know God is to *know* salvation (John 6:29 and 17:23), and to *experience* Christ in salvation by the work of the Spirit. And in this, God ordered his church to set apart officers for the lower degrees of ministration to aid people on the celestial journey to heaven to know the Savior, so elders were "ordained...in every church," who were acknowledged to be "made overseers over the flock" by the appointment of the Holy Spirit.[6] God has ordained three sources for the communication of his truth. In the (1) Scriptures he has preserved it by his providence against all hostile attacks. In (2) the hearts of Christians he has

---

[3] Murphy, Thomas, *Pastoral Theology,* (Audubon, NJ: Old Paths Publications, 1996) 37.
[4] Murphy, Ibid, 38.
[5] Murphy, Ibid, pages 38-39.
[6] See Acts 6:1-6, 14:23, 20:28.

maintained it by the Almighty power of his Spirit —
even under every outward indication of general
apostasy. And (3) in the ministry of the watchman he
has he deposited "the treasure in earthen vessels" for the
edification and enriching of the church in successive
ages.[7] And so, the watchman must acknowledge how
solemn his sanction is — infinitely above all human
authority — which is stamped and engraved on the
sacred office. And how tremendous the guilt of rejecting
its commission!

    The church is to represent the dignity of the Son
of God, and watchmen, then, are entrusted to watch the
church on behalf of King Jesus with the Gospel which
reflects the divine glory of the God-Man in his work and
merit. Such entrusted power must be stirred up and
worked out in the life of the pastor.[8] They are set up in
Christ's church as watchmen for the glory of God and
the good of the flock. The ministry is "winning souls"
and the minister must say "this is the one work I do." He
must, then, focus his whole heart and life on the pulpit.[9]
This is not an easy task, and should not be taken lightly.
William Taylor says, "If, therefore, young gentlemen,
you have chosen the ministry, expecting to be carried to
heaven "on flowery beds of ease," you have made an
egregious mistake."[10] The Gospel ministry is *work*. It

---

[7] Bridges, Ibid. 4.
[8] *cf.* 1 Tim. 4:14; 2 Tim. 1:6.
[9] Taylor, William M., *The Ministry of the Word*, (Harrisburg, PA: Sprinkle Publications, 2003) 2.
[10] Ibid, 8.

requires putting on habits which will cause success, which in itself is a hard work. The ministry is primarily and pre-eminently a work of service to God, for the people. Taylor says, "The people are not for the minister, but the minister is for the people; and he is to lose himself in their service and for their benefit."[11] The office of the preacher is that of a helper of his fellows. His special duty is to lead them to Christ who is their Helper and Redeemer, and to assist them in the understanding of his word, and in the application of its principles to their daily lives. Such a watchman holds steadfastly that he is there *for the flock*, and self-renunciation is the root of excellence in his office. Everything that the watchman does comes down to *speech* in some way or another. The watchman takes the word, and applies that to various duties in his pastoral office: the ministry of the word in preaching and prayer, and the ministry of the word in visitation, catechizing, comforting, admonishing, discipline and the like, are all applications of the word.

Primarily, we see the watchman's description and qualifications (as well as ability) in such passages as Job 33:23, Jeremiah 3:6-15, Ezekiel 33:1-9, 1 Timothy 3 and Titus 1, among others. In passages like these, the marks show a *mature* man of God. It is a very dangerous and difficult office to take on, knowing that every minute of their consecrated life is set before God as one *leading* Christ's sheep on behalf of the sovereign God of the universe. They are under great attacks from the devil;

---

[11] Ibid., 13.

they have grave responsibilities before Christ the King as watchman, and they must be solemnly set in their duty by the power of the Holy Spirit, without which, as we see so often, they miscarry in their undertaking before King Jesus. Nathaniel Vincent said, "Many ministers miscarry. Many fall into hell from under the pulpit, and out of the pulpit; they are able to preach to others, and yet themselves are castaways."[12]

Do you believe *you* are a pastor? You may be *in* the office of a pastor, but do you believe you have been called and gifted by Jesus Christ to be his watchman? Do you believe you have been called *to* the ministry? How do you *know* you are a pastor? Here is a helpful test: do you think, as ministers measure up, that you are one in a thousand? I hope you believe that in truth. Ministers are supposed to be 1 in 1000 in terms of their effectiveness. Yes, *literally*. That's what Elihu said to Job, "If there be a messenger with him, an interpreter, one among a thousand, to shew unto man his uprightness: Then he is gracious unto him, and saith, Deliver him from going down to the pit: I have found a ransom," (Job. 33:23-24). William Perkins in his work, *The Calling of the Ministry*, said that there is no reason in the passage on Job 33 that we are not to take it literally, 1 in 1000.[13] So, are you 1 in 1000?

---

[12] Vincent, Nathaniel, *A Discourse on Self-Examination*, (Coconut Creek: 2013, Puritan Publications), 91.
[13] "This can be taken either literally or figuratively. In the figurative sense, it is true of ministers in and of themselves; in the strict, literal sense, the comparison is with all men. According to the figurative,

The 1647 Westminster Confession of Faith states, "The officers which Christ hath appointed for the edification of his church, and the perfecting of the saints, are, some extraordinary, as apostles, evangelists, and prophets, which are ceased. Others ordinary and perpetual, as pastors, teachers, and other church-governors, and deacons."[14] Consider, *Christ the King* appoints *the office*. Perpetual and ordinary offices are pastors, teachers, and other church-governors, and deacons.[15] Charles Bridges presses ministers to rely, then, on the power of Christ for success in being a faithful watchman in this office, "Let us, then, adopt as our own, the words of that most eminent servant of God, Moses, when praying for the display of the Divine power and glory to his people Israel, "Make us glad according to the days wherein thou hast afflicted us, and the years wherein we have seen evil. Let thy work appear unto thy servants, and thy glory unto their children. Let the beauty of the Lord our God be upon us; and establish thou the work of our hands upon us; yea, the work of our

---

hyperbolical sense; among all ministers, not one of many is a right angel and a true interpreter. According to the plain and literal sense; among the men of this world, there is not one in a thousand who proves to be a true minister." Perkins, William, eBook, *The Calling of the Ministry*, (Crossville, TN: Puritan Publications, 2017) chapter 2.

[14] Presbyterian Form of Government, Westminster Standards.

[15] See the *Form of Presbyterial Church Government* for Scriptural Rules Concerning Ordination such as ordaining Ministers, the Doctrine of Ordination, the Power of Ordination, the Doctrinal Part of Ordination of Ministers, the Rules for Examination and Extraordinary Practices.

hands establish thou it.""[16] God must make *the success* in pastoral ministry, but he gifts watchman as those secondary causes which are to be used in the ministry to establish his will in the life of the people.

The somber and grave level of seriousness in ministerial commitment needed to function biblically in the office of the watchman is all but lost in our day. For a contemporary "pastor," their main objective is often to be the people's *friend* instead of the one sent to the people by God to, "show a man his righteousness." Bible knowledge in general has been placed at the wayside making room for *sharing sessions* on "Sunday morning" (not the Lord's Day from their perspective) instead of preaching the word and sounding the alarm. Today the criteria for pastor or elder is not 1 Timothy 3 and Titus 1, but rather the marketing strategy and some kind of manufactured CEO talent which may be prevalent in the "job applicant" in a church that is "purpose driven" to grow into a congregation of thousands. Many Pastors do not even know the books of the bible, or read through the whole bible! Many of them have *never* read a historical confession, or are even vaguely familiar with historical theology. Very few men are really qualified to minister to God's chosen people, and care for the flock of Christ *even though* they have been through seminary. "My people have been lost sheep. Their shepherds have lead them astray," (Jeremiah 50:6a). Seminary graduates

---

[16] Bridges, Charles, *The Christian Ministry*, (London: R.B. Seeley and W. Burnside, 1830) 660.

often lead people astray because they are not yet fit for the ministry.

What is the, "nature of the oversight for the watchman?" Richard Baxter makes notations concerning unfit ministers, or those who are parading wolves in sheep's clothing. He says, "To bear with the vices of the ministry is to promote the ruin of the church; for what speedier way is there for the depraving and undoing of the people, than the depravity of their guides?"[17] In other words, even in Baxter's time, (and I think no less in our own), ministers are often preachers before they are Christians. They do not have a life *consecrated* to God first. Their lives, their speech, their actions, their families, their children, do not show forth a life consecrated to God; they look like the world, dressed up in ministerial garb. They will know the latest movies, and their children will be sound in their understanding of how to play video games, but ask them to explain *justification by faith*, and they may give you a blank stare.

The watchman is to *sound the alarm* for God's people as the voice of the Lord. God says such pastors will *do something* which is spiritually important for the good of the church in Jeremiah 3:15, "And I will give you pastors according to mine heart, which shall *feed you* with knowledge and understanding." What do they do on behalf of the Great Shepherd? "...they will feed you."

---

[17] Baxter, Richard, *The Reformed Pastor*, (eBook, Christian Classics Ethereal Library, Grand Rapids, MI) 2.

A shepherd's purpose is to tend and feed the sheep. He loves to feed the sheep. Not because he is forced to, but rather, because he has a heart after God's own heart; he loves to do it! The desire of this feeder is to feed as God would feed. And how does he do it? "...with knowledge." What is the form of this food that feeders feed? It is the knowledge of the word, and knowledge of God. *Knowledge* is information about something. These feeders are to feed the sheep of Judah with *knowledge*. What kind of knowledge? Farming? Construction? Military strategy? No; knowledge of God as Father, Son and Spirit, and how to have true and lasting communion with God in eternal life! Watchmen feed God's people with the knowledge of God; but they do not stop with just supplying this knowledge, because it is not merely the regurgitation of biblical material that God is after. Anyone can memorize facts about the bible. Instead, feeders, feed them with knowledge, "and understanding." Another word for "understanding" is "insight." It is connected to *wisdom*. Wisdom is the *right* application of knowledge. It's not enough for God's people to be catechized according to knowledge, just to *know about* God, but they should *apply* what they know correctly. If Aaron, the high priest, knows *how* to offer the sacrifice on the altar for the forgiveness of the sins of the Israelites, but he does not *go and do* the sacrifice the right way, the knowledge is *useless*; as much as if one knows that Christ beckons sinners to come to him for rest, and yet they do not go to Christ for rest, the knowledge is useless for the benefit of the one knowing. God's meaning is, watchmen who have the same interests that God does, who will feed his people with knowledge about him and the various ways to apply that knowledge, this is done so that that they might not be rebellious and defiant sinners. They will be his beloved people according to holiness. Watchmen in this way, *after God's own heart,* are a demonstration of his promised mercy. The church has been given Christ's ordained minister to exemplify *his* heart according to God's knowledge for the instruction of God's people. Watchmen must be *very, very good* at sounding the alarm in this. Keep in mind, God is the True Shepherd; Ezekiel 34:11-31 shows this plainly. "Woe to the shepherds of Israel who feed themselves! Should not the shepherds feed the flocks?" (Ezek. 34:2). "Indeed I Myself will search for My sheep and seek them out," (Ezek. 34:11). "I seek out My sheep and deliver them," (Ezek. 34:12). "I will bring them out," (Ezek. 34:13). "I will feed them," (Ezek. 34:13). "I will make them lie down," (Ezek. 34:15). "I will seek what was lost and bring back what was driven away, bind up the broken and strengthen what was sick," (Ezek. 34:16). "I will save My flock," (Ezek. 34:22). "I will establish one shepherd over them, and he shall feed them...I will make a covenant of peace with them," (Ezek. 34:23-25). Watchmen are to be under-shepherds according to God's heart in the same way. Such watchmen are to preach the word, (sound the alarm), give attendance to

13

reading, to exhortation, to doctrine, take heed to himself, and take heed of the flock which he is made overseer. It is not an office which can be regarded lightly. Thomas Murphy said, "A very high appreciation of his office is one of the first qualifications for him who would be an efficient pastor."[18] This means to esteem the office is to esteem the work of the office, which is set in glorifying God in preaching and ministering the word. Murphy says, "Ministers, especially younger ones, should regard the acquisition of knowledge as to the duties of their office as one of their most important pursuits."[19] Why? To minister this word to others. How will a minister be able to oversee or lead the flock without the knowledge to do so? It is not only an ordering of what is to be learned or known, but what must be daily put into practice. What a grave responsibility it is to be set as a watchman over the city of God!

It may be that you are *not* a minister of the Gospel and are reading this work to study the biblical nature of a watchman. Certainly, this work will be a help in this way. To know what God requires as God's voice in the church, is to be informed about the kind of minister or watchman your church *should have* (Malachi 2:1-9); that your church has a watchman who

---

[18] Murphy, Thomas, *Pastoral Theology*, (Audubon, NJ: Old Paths Publications, 1996) 27.
[19] Murphy, 34.

preaches the word boldly, plainly and faithfully.[20] Our first task in this is to set down the nature of a watchman, and focus in on his work. So, *let's get started.*

---

[20] See my work, *The Lord's Voice Cries in the City*, for a full discussion of this point.

Chapter 1:
What is a Watchman?

"Again the word of the LORD came unto me, saying, Son of man, speak to the children of thy people, and say unto them, When I bring the sword upon a land, if the people of the land take a man of their coasts, and set him for their watchman: If when he seeth the sword come upon the land, he blow the trumpet, and warn the people; Then whosoever heareth the sound of the trumpet, and taketh not warning; if the sword come, and take him away, his blood shall be upon his own head. He heard the sound of the trumpet, and took not warning; his blood shall be upon him. But he that taketh warning shall deliver his soul. But if the watchman see the sword come, and blow not the trumpet, and the people be not warned; if the sword come, and take any person from among them, he is taken away in his iniquity; but his blood will I require at the watchman's hand. So thou, O son of man, I have set thee a watchman unto the house of Israel; therefore thou shalt hear the word at my mouth, and warn them from me. When I say unto the wicked, O wicked man, thou shalt surely die; if thou dost not speak to warn the wicked from his way, that wicked man shall die in his iniquity; but his blood will I require at thine hand. Nevertheless, if thou warn the wicked of his way to turn from it; if he do not turn from his way, he shall die in his iniquity; but thou hast delivered thy soul," (Ezek. 33:1-9).

We begin this study with Ezekiel 33 and the confirmation of the prophet's work. The restoration of Israel from bondage is seen from Ezekiel 33 to 39. But in Ezekiel 33, which is where out text lies, there is a restatement of the prophet's call (verses 1-9) and a confirmation of the prophet's work (verses 10-20). There is also annexed to this a criticism in judgment against those not repentant (verses 21ff).

Ezekiel 33 may be divided into three parts in this way: a warning to heed the watchman (verses 1–9); an exhortation for the people to turn from wickedness and evil ways (verses 10–20); and, Jerusalem's fall and Israel's failure to listen to God (verses 21–33).

Verses 1-9 are a kind of repetition of an earlier section of Ezekiel in 3:16-21. There Ezekiel was first appointed as the "watchman over" the church (3:17). It recounts the principle of "the watchman" from Ezekiel 3 in 33:1–6 and names Ezekiel as the church's watchman in verses 7–9 *restating* his commission.

So far, from the beginning of the book until chapter 33 Ezekiel had fulfilled what God was requiring of him as a watchman. He was set to call God's people to repentance in the context of his office as a watchman lest God's judgment reign down upon his house (which judgment comes in verse 21). "The city is smitten," (Ezek. 33:21). If people do not listen to the watchman, their death is their own fault. Ezekiel, as a watchman was without guilt if he sounds the trumpet, the alarm, even if no one reacts as they should. But Ezekiel would be *very* guilty if people perished as a result of his negligence in *not* sounding the alarm when the attack was present (verses 5–6).

In military matters, cities were built with towers on the walls where watchmen would lookout (*cf.* Isa. 21:5). If impending attack was to occur, they would sound the alarm. The "trumpet," the *shofar*, ram's horn, was used to sound the warning and alarm the people of an attack. "If when he seeth the sword come upon the land, he blow the trumpet, and warn the people," (Ezek. 33:3). This horn is seen in Scripture for both military and religious purposes. "And seven priests shall bear before the ark seven trumpets of rams' horns: and the seventh day ye shall compass the city seven times, and the priests shall blow with the trumpets," (Joshua 6:4). "O my soul, the sound of the trumpet, the alarm of war," (Jer. 4:19).[1] Ezekiel, the watchman, is *commissioned by God* to blow the "trumpet," sounding the alarm to warn of impending judgment, and in this case, physical war, which God would use against his people for their sin, and it metaphorically enhances the idea of *spiritual war* on sin and wickedness. For, in reality, physical war is tied to spiritual wickedness or repelled by spiritual holiness.

The message of the trumpet, the *metaphor* of the trumpet, Ezekiel's "alarm," were warnings that God gave specifically to him, and were of divine origin. "...therefore thou shalt hear the word at my mouth, and warn them from me," (Ezek. 33:7). He is God's spokesman, he is

---

[1] See also 2 Sam. 2:28; Psa. 81:3; Joel 2:15; Amos 3:6; Hosea 5:8.

God's messenger, he is God's *watchman*. As if God said to him, "Listen and obey the speaking of *my* mouth and tell them for me what I tell you to tell them." This interesting twist on the idea of the watchman is not set in just looking with the eyes from a tower and using his own power to scan out whether enemies were coming. Ezekiel was the messenger of a *divine word;* at this point in history, it was orally dictated to him by God (though written down for us). When God spoke to him, Ezekiel would then speak to the people, and he would deliver the message God had given him in its *exactness* and *entirety* and this would then fulfill what God set him to do.

Ezekiel is called out again as *son of man*, to be a watchman, a man *of the people*, to speak to God's people (fallen people). He is to speak to the church of the day, those people of the same covenantal responsibility as he was. In Hebrew, the phrase means to speak to "the sons of your people." William Greenhill on this text here said that is very important to note that God had disowned the Israelites for their sin and calls them not, "the children of my people," but, "to thy people," speaking to Ezekiel.[2] This kind of language occurs in 3:11; 13:17; 33:2, 12, 17, 30; in all these verses it is "the children of thy people." This is like when a wife says to her husband, "do you know what your son did today?" When the Israelites sinned in making the golden calf, the same

---

[2] Greenhill, William, *An Exposition of the Prophet on Ezekiel*, see chapter 33.

phrase, "And the LORD said unto Moses, Go, get thee down; for thy people, which thou broughtest out of the land of Egypt, have corrupted themselves," (Exod. 32:7; Deut. 9:12) is used. God uses the same language in Hosea 4: because of all their swearing, lying, killing, stealing, committing adultery, ... (Hosea 4:2). It is always used in this fashion as it related to covenant breaking and sin.

Ezekiel is posted as a watchman by God. The word "watchman" literally means "to observe, to open the eyes, and fix the eyes to see and understand its object." It is to take *special notice* of something. "...and the watchman went up to the roof over the gate unto the wall, and lifted up his eyes, and looked, and behold a man running alone," (2 Sam. 18:24). Or, "Go, set a watchman, let him declare what he seeth," (Isa. 21:6). This is to be spiritually minded, Christ says to his disciples, "Take ye heed, watch and pray," (Mark 13:33). Further implications of what he says to his disciples is also applied to all by way of extension. "And what I say unto you I say unto all, watch," (Mark 13:37). As if he says, "Set yourself in such a way as to make a sure discovery of the things you behold, and intently understand and know their implications." A *commissioned* watchman warns, "if when he seeth the sword come upon the land," *etc.*

This verse in Ezekiel sets out the official office of the watchman. He is to watch to see if there is any danger approaching. If he sees anything to be done for the protection of the people, he is to blow the trumpet.

He is to give them warning in order to stir up any actions that would enhance the church's well-being. Such blowing of the trumpet, some Hebrew scholars say, comes from a phrase meaning to *shine* or *illuminate,* in Hebrew. If the watchman does his job, he illuminates, *shines* the importance of the alarm, and he has done his job, where the guilt of blood is not on his hands if the people do not listen to him. If the watchman does not do his job, and does not warn the people of impending attack, and neglects his office (as God orders), he is guilty of bloodshed, which is a *capital crime* against the people. "But if the watchman see the sword come, and blow not the trumpet, and the people be not warned..." which states that all watchmen are *not* faithful; some are lazy and careless and negligent to their own damnation.

The Lord sets this watchman in his place. He is to know what God says, specifically, to know the word, alarm sinners of the word, and help them to see what sin and righteousness are, what punishments or blessings might come, what God's wrath is or his divine favor in his covenant, and such things. He is to tell the people, not by things *he makes up,* or what he thinks they want to hear, but by what God has *already said* in Scripture, or at this time in the church's history; what Ezekiel would receive directly from the mouth of God and carrying of the Holy Spirit.[3]

---

[3] "For the prophecy came not in old time by the will of man: but holy men of God spake as they were moved by the Holy Ghost," (2 Peter 1:21). They had, "the Spirit of Christ which was in them..." (1 Peter 1:11).

What did God tell him to do in all this? He said, "And warn them from me." Ezekiel as a watchman must not speak to the people in his own name, but the voice of the Lord cries in the mouth of the prophet. "The LORD'S voice cries to the city and the man of wisdom shall see your name: "Hear the rod! Who has appointed it?" (Micah 6:9).

Make note of this, God alone has the authority to set watchmen over his church. Only God can make a watchman over his church, a minister of the Gospel. The watchman and minister are one and the same in this light. God alone is the Author of all offices in the church whether they are extraordinary or ordinary, and no man ought to come into any of them without a direct commission from God, called to church-work according to God's will. They are to be called to the office for a specific need in the church. The watchmen are responsible before God, and for the people. The watchman's life is a life of consecration to this. It is being called by a special calling of God for a special purpose of God. The watchmen is first converted, and then commissioned. First, Ezekiel ate, "And he said unto me, Son of man, cause thy belly to eat, and fill thy bowels with this roll that I give thee. Then did I eat it; and it was in my mouth as honey for sweetness," (Ezek. 3:3). Then he preached. Carnal men find no sweetness in the word, nor in God's Christ. Ezekiel had ingested the word, and the Spirit of God had lifted him up on it and in it. "And the Spirit entered into me when he spake unto me, and set me upon my feet, that I heard him that spake unto me," (Ezek. 2:2). Watchmen who are commissioned of God, who know the sweetness of his word, hear his voice clearly. Christ says, "My sheep hear my voice, and I know them, and they follow me," (John 10:27).

What does a call to the office of a watchman "sound like" today? Consider first, in Ezekiel's day, God, by way of theophany, came and called him to the task; there was no choice for Ezekiel, as there was no choice for running Jonah, who was brought back to his commission by a hurricane and a great fish that swallowed him (Jonah 1:15, 17). But now that God *has spoken* (past tense) in his word, and it is written down,[4] how does the Spirit of God separate Paul and Barnabas for the work of the ministry, to be watchman (Acts 13:2)? How does that call, or what does that call, look like? "To exercise legitimately the ministry, we must have been called to it."[5] There is no legitimate exercise to the ministry if God has not called a person to be in the ministry. Without an internal call and an external call they *cannot be* in the ministry; in this way, without an internal call from God, one cannot with safety begin the work of Christ's ministry. Do ministers today actually believe that? Many think all they need is a piece of paper that says they took some classes at seminary. Is *that* what makes a minister?

---

[4] "All scripture is given by inspiration of God, and is profitable for doctrine, for reproof, for correction, for instruction in righteousness," (2 Tim. 3:16).
[5] Vinet, *Pastoral Theology*, eBook, chapter 7.

The minister, the watchman, acts in the name of another, that is, of God, who has called him to the task of *watching*. He is commissioned by God with supernatural gifts which allow him to discern, speak and work in the ministry by the word. He officiates in that office and so he must be sent by God. So, it follows that anyone in the office has no warrant for relying on divine aid and favor unless God has sent them. They can never claim blessings on what they have not been given if God has not sent them.

In our day, the call to be a watchman in the ministry evidences itself, like every other aspect of the church, by ordinary means, under the direction of the word and Spirit of God. In this call, if watchmen desire to attain clearness in their call, they should combine circumstances and principles which have been established by good sense and the providence of God in the church; internally by God and externally by the people of the church. That means the word of God in the qualification of the office is essential, and the providences around them show that the need and the opportunity in the church are both essential. No one is ever called to an office in the church merely by their own outward calling or desire. God must call them and commission them. Scripturally, watchmen can be called by immediate revelation, as with the prophets, where God showed up and spoke directly to them (consider Ezekiel in our text, and Isaiah in Isaiah 6). Or, they are called by an agreement of Scriptural rules directing them to the ministry in the church. At the same time, they are directed by some outward acts of providence, which are necessary to be commissioned to the office; which is why we say there *must be a need*. Surely, the prophet Jeremiah had an infallible assurance of the author of his message, when he pleaded for himself before the princes, "Of a truth the LORD hath sent me unto you to speak all these words in your ears," (Jeremiah 26:15). This the watchman *always* says. "God has sent me."

Ministers in times past have used certain ideas, questions and statements to "flush out" whether or not someone believes they are called to the ministry to be a watchman for God. Alexander Vinet used these questions:

> Can you adopt, as expressing your self-consecration, these words of St. Paul: "And all things are of God, who hath reconciled us to himself by Jesus Christ, and hath given to us the ministry of reconciliation. To wit, that God was in Christ, reconciling the world to himself, not imputing their trespasses unto them, and hath committed to us the word of reconciliation. Now then we are ambassadors for Christ, as though God did beseech you by us: we pray you in Christ's stead, be ye reconciled to God," (2 Cor. 5:18-20)? Do you have in your heart any measure of the feeling which St. Paul expresses when he says, "My little children, of whom I travail in

birth till Christ be formed in you," (Gal. 4:19)? With your whole heart do you receive this precept of the apostle, "Let the same mind be in you which was also in Christ Jesus, who, being in the form of God, thought it not robbery to be equal with God, but made himself of no reputation, and took upon him the form of a servant," (Phil. 2:5-7)? Do you enter fully and freely into the thought, "I fill up that which is behind of the afflictions of Christ, in my flesh, for his body's sake, which is the Church?"[6]

Charles Bridges asks of ministers in office to consider these questions:

"Do we honor our work? Do we feel the responsibility of our work? What is our personal sympathy with this awful sense of responsibility? How do we feel with regard to our talents? How does our public example speak as a most responsible part of our office to the church? Do we earnestly desire and expect success in our work? Are we laying ourselves out for our work? Does the Spirit of love characterize our work? Do we pray diligently for our flock?"[7]

---

[6] Vinet, Ibid. chapter 1.
[7] Bridges, Ibid, 628.

A call to the ministry in the form of a *desire* springs from love; and yes, from ambition too, but ambition for God and the desire of God's glory to be seen in the people and in the church. The watchman is to be at least ready in his submission to whatever in the ministry is laborious, painful, humiliating, and even what he might think is of small importance. Is the watchman ready for *this*, as much as they *desire* those important aspects as laboring in the word and prayer as inclinations of their mind? Watchmen find the office, even amidst difficulty, as excellent, and something to be highly esteemed.

What is a "watchman" from this biblical perspective? Ezekiel, as with all God's ministers, was set apart by God. It is quite conclusive in the passage, that he is "set" as a watchman. *God* does this; and he does it through Jesus Christ, who is the Shepherd and Bishop of souls. "For ye were as sheep going astray; but are now returned unto the Shepherd and Bishop of your souls," (1 Peter 2:25) ... yes, but how? Christ, "*gave* some, apostles; and some, prophets; and some, evangelists; and some, pastors and teachers," (Eph. 4:11). God alone makes watchmen and sets them over his church by the power of the Spirit that discerns the gifts and graces he gives to members of his church; men do not *make* themselves in this way. Take Isaiah; Isaiah was afraid in his meeting with Christ (John 12:41 and Isaiah 6). Such fear is not limited to just Isaiah. In every passage that men come into contact with God, they become reverently fearful for themselves and the never dying souls of the people. If watchmen ever aim to be made instruments of God's glory in saving souls, then at the outset they should set before their eyes not the honor but the *danger* of their calling. Isaiah pronounces a curse on himself, "Woe is me, for I am undone." This is what he said in Isaiah 6 when he met with King Jesus seated on the throne and was commissioned to be a preacher, a watchman, for the church. God first humbled the prophet in the sight of Christ's majesty. He shows him his own misery and the misery of the people. And before he honors him with a commission to preach his word to his people as a watchman, Isaiah's says, "I am a man of unclean lips." He complains of sinfulness before God; his unworthiness. Isaiah is not only unclean himself, but is sent to an unclean people. This is because he, "dwells," with them, knowing them, as a watchman must be among the people of God; not aloof, not distant, but among them; in their lives.[8] And, consider, that which prompted Isaiah's uncleanness and confession was a vision of a holy God. Men ought to consider the extreme presumption of rashly entering the ministry in this light

---

[8] Church members today often have never experienced what it means for a watchman *to watch over them* and be "in" their lives (especially in more "independent" countries today that breed independent Christians). They are content enough, without experience, to come to church when they want, and *maybe* have the pastor pray over them once a year for two minutes. This is not the function of the watchman. Biblical watchmen are in the lives of their people, they dwell with them, know their needs, know their sins, know their afflictions, etc., so they can be a help to them, and they can seek the law in their mouth (Mal. 2:7).

alone; they serve a holy God and they are to be a mouthpiece for him to the people.

There are three designations to consider of the *watchman* in Scripture as it relates to his office. Let's consider them to gain a greater gravity of the work. The first is "messenger," (or angel), showing God's word must be spoken, and it must be spoken as God's word. "And unto the angel of the church," (Rev. 2:8). "Behold, I send my messenger before thy face," (Matt. 11:10). In this way watchmen show their faithfulness to the Lord in sincerely discharging the message which he has honored them to carry. They magnify Christ through the Spirit of God, and not themselves, in their preaching of his Word, (which is the exact opposite of most modern evangelical preachers today who want to tell the congregation stories and illustrations about their life). As a note which we will consider in the next chapter, in preaching as a watchman, there is also an important application to hearers, who should hear the preacher gladly, willingly, reverently and obediently.

The second is, an "interpreter." "If there be a messenger with him, an interpreter, one among a thousand, to shew unto man his uprightness," (Job 33:23). He is someone who is able to deliver the reconciliation made between God and man, who knows the words of God's mouth and delivers that word boldly, faithfully and plainly. He must be able to expound and explain the God of the covenant, the Christ of the covenant, and the grace of the covenant, and rightly lay down how this reconciliation, is accomplished in the power of the Spirit. Such an interpreter must have a form of learning, divine knowledge, inwardly taught and instructed by the Spirit of God as much as outwardly taught. William Perkins said, "How can anyone be God's interpreter to his people unless he knows the mind of God himself?"[9]

Thirdly, the watchman is also "one in a thousand." Again, "If there be a messenger with him, an interpreter, one among a thousand, to shew unto man his uprightness," (Job 33:23). Put it to theoretical use – and gather up 1000 and only one can be found to truly show a man his uprightness. There are in fact very *few* watchmen. If watchmen are so scarce, the church must be exhorted to take great care not to decrease their number. Instead, they ought all they can to increase their number for the glory of God and the good of the church. If watchmen are few in number, then the church must do all it can to increase their number by God's grace for the good of the harvest, which, currently, is very plentiful. Did not Christ say to, "pray the Lord of the harvest, to send out laborers into his harvest," (Luke 10:2)? These are his watchmen.

What, then, constitutes a *call* to be a watchman for Christ in the ministry? It is both internal and external. Concerning the one desiring the office of a minister or watchman, the operation of divine grace on their souls, coupled with something they believe to be

---

[9] Perkins, Ibid, chapter 2.

true about their life-experience, they feel moved with a resolute strength to give themselves to the holy call. The actual ministry of the one desiring the office is considered in the testimony it bears outwardly. The minister should take heed to himself that he is both called and sent by God to the task of the Gospel, the good news that God gives him as one who must sound an alarm, to behold the people, know their spiritual and physical needs, and apply that word rightly to them.

It sometimes helps to clarify a man's call to the ministry, that there has been a conscientious diligence in all the means of being fit for the work itself. Being *fit* for the work of the ministry is a great proof of a man's call to it. Keep in mind, the Lord calls no man to a work for which he does not qualify him, especially in this as a watchman over the never-dying souls of his church.

Those that are called to office by God in the church are then to be set as watchmen. But the importance of this statement is lost without understanding what a watchman or minister actually is. In other words, there are certain uncompromising marks that attend a godly watchman for Christ. Again, to reiterate, these marks demonstrate a man's capacity to lead others in the Christian life, having spiritual maturity as one who also continually leads his own family, causing them to discernably grow, and conforms them further to the image of Jesus Christ day to day. His life is consecrated, his family is consecrated, his household in its entirety is consecrated and everything he does is given in service to King Jesus. It's what a professing Christian should do, but it includes all that a true Christian is and how to lead others into the same effectively by the graces of the Holy Spirit.[10] In the New Testament this is *almost* comprehensibly explained in 1 Timothy 3 and Titus 1, where the marks are listed which demonstrate a mature man of God (though Old Testament references are equally important to the life and work of the watchman). Here I will merely list for you the non-negotiable qualifications for a watchman that God calls to the ministry so that you are familiar with what the Scriptures teach concerning this, with a short note on each one.

Desire (1 Tim. 3:1). It is a "noble task" to desire the ministry of Jesus Christ. This is where the godly, qualified man of God desires above all things to be a minister in the duties of public preaching, prayer, and pastoral theology.

Blameless (1 Tim. 3:2, 1 Tim. 3:10, Titus 1:6-7). The watchman will be "without reproach" in the eyes of the church. All men are often without reproach in their own eyes, but "blameless" speaks to the perception of those in the church.

He is the husband of one wife (1 Tim. 3:2). This is a solemn faithfulness to his wife; he is a man, not a woman; the *husband* of one wife. In Roman times polygamy would have been acceptable among *Romans;*

---

[10] See my work, *Walking Victoriously in the Power of the Spirit*, for a full discussion of this point.

where the representative before the flock of God, the watchman of the church, is to be a "one woman man." It is a command against polygamy, as well as against being flirtatious. He is dedicated to his wife alone.

Vigilant (1 Tim. 3:11, Titus 2:2). The watchman is to have both self-control, and is to be sober in his watchfulness both over his own piety and the holiness of the church. So much so that zeal is described as vigilant for the cause of holiness.

Sober (1 Tim. 3:2). The watchman is to be of a sound mind, self-controlled, sober-minded, moderate in all his ways, discreet, prudent and sensible; this is meaning of the word *sober.*

Of good behavior (1 Tim. 3:2). The watchman is orderly, decent, modest, honorable, virtuous, and respectable in the eyes of the people.

Given to hospitality (1 Tim. 3:2). The watchman is hospitable, one who loves to care for strangers, and who loves the fellowship and holy conversation of the flock.

Apt to teach (1 Tim. 3:2). Watchmen are to be skilled in teaching, apt to it, *capable.* This does not mean he is "instantly" a seminary professor because he went to seminary and regurgitated information back to his professors to get a degree, but he does have the quality of being able to teach the Gospel, and silence the gainsayer against it; to encourage and teach the saints the mystery of godliness and the salvation to be found only in Jesus Christ.

Patient (1 Tim. 3:3). Patient means forbearing, both with himself and others. The watchman should be patient with the flock of God knowing sanctification is the work of the Holy Spirit.

A good husband and father (1 Tim. 3:4; Titus 1:6). The watchman is one that rules his own house well, having his children in subjection, with all gravity and having faithful children not accused of riot or unruly behavior; equally, he is to be a husband like *Christ is to the church,* to his wife.

A good witness (1 Tim. 3:7). The watchman will have a good witness by the evidence of his life outside and inside the church. His life is a proof of what a "good reputation" means as it is laid out all through the book of Proverbs; he is a shining example of a good reputation.

Faithful (noted in 2 Tim. 2:2). The watchman is a believer of the gospel, and can be trusted with the office as ambassador before God and men as one who keeps his dedication and promises to work as, "unto the Lord."

A lover of good men (Titus 1:8). The watchman promotes virtue, and loves that which is good, both in what men do and who they are.

Just (Titus 1:8). The watchman is fair and unbiased in his judgement with those inside and outside the church in all things.

Holy (Titus 1:8). The watchman is consecrated to God, has an eminent pious devotion to God, is pure from being defiled, and in a relationship with God that demonstrates true piety to others.

Temperate (Titus 1:8). The watchman is self-controlled (Gal. 5 as a fruit of the Spirit); and holds the highest morals in relation to the Law of God.

A man of conviction (Titus 1:9), one who holds unswervingly to the accepted Christian truth of God's word. The watchman holds fast the Word of God that he has been taught, having a unified conviction in his sound doctrine with those before him, to exhort and to convince the gainsayer, console those who are bruised by the world, and can oppose false teachers and heretics, while comforting and encouraging the godly.

These qualifications encompass that which the watchman cannot do without. For 1 Timothy 3 and Titus 1 are non-negotiable for the watchman. The watchman must sensibly and discernably exemplify these things, which places him in the category of a mature Christian believer; *both he and his family.*

As much as there are positive traits which show themselves in the minister or watchman, there should also be taken into consideration the negative traits, or negative descriptors, that Paul gives which also disqualify one from the office, those attributes of sin which the watchman cannot live in or with. These are those which would disqualify him from the ministry. These are:

Being given to drunkenness (1 Tim. 3:3). This means that the watchman is not given over to an addictive personality. Being violent (1 Tim. 3:3). Being greedy for power (1 Tim. 3:3). Being argumentative (1 Tim. 3:3). Being a lover of money (1 Tim. 3:3). Being a novice or new convert (1 Tim. 3:6). This is an extremely important, but almost a repetitive point that Paul gives, which shows its importance, since none of the qualifications or disqualifications could be given to someone *who is a novice.* It would require a seasoned watchman, or one who is seasoned in the ways of the office, and as a Christian, and of knowledge to the word of God which God commissions them to teach others. Being self-willed (Titus 1:7); for he does not serve himself but God and the people. Being easily angered (Titus 1:7). Seeing these as the over-arching culmination of the watchman's ministry, it would behoove all Christians to take these into account in either considering the ministry, and looking for an elder under Christ for the ministry; every male in the church should consider whether they ought to be in the ministry or not since the harvest is plentiful.

But these qualifications, all of them, are non-negotiable (whether positive or negative), the positive traits must be present, though not perfect. They are not advisements, good advice, or mere suggestions. They are *qualifications* of God's watchman. The church in all its ways is to represent the dignity of the Son of God, which includes the work of the ministry under the one who watches the church for glory of Christ. Watchmen, then, are entrusted with the Gospel which reflects the divine glory of the God-Man Jesus Christ, and the need to demonstrate, from their very person, the dignity of the office which represents the Christ; they are not merely *sharing* a Sunday school lesson. Such entrusting power must be stirred up and worked out in the life of the pastor (cf. 1 Tim. 4:14; 2 Tim. 1:6). Charles Bridges said, "A sense of the dignity of our office — accurately formed, carefully maintained, and habitually exercised — is therefore of the highest importance."[11] And rightly, John Newton said, "None but he who made the world can make a minister of the Gospel."[12] Those who are made such will be discernable to the biblical eye.

The two primary duties of the watchman are preaching and prayer. Ezekiel was instructed by God to give the precise word that God gave to his prophet to give to the people. Listen now, and weigh preachers by Ezekiel today: Ezekiel did not have a license to shorten the word God gave him. He did not have license to expand it. He did not have license to change it. As *God's* mouthpiece, the watchman's main occupation is prayer and the ministry of God's word. This equates to power and guidance for the people of God.

He is required by God for the good of the church to watch and pray. This is what Christ told his ministers. "Watch and pray," (Matt. 26:41). "Take ye heed, watch and pray," (Mark 13:33). "Watch ye and

---

[11] Bridges, Ibid, 10.
[12] Newton, John, *The Works of John Newton*, Volume 5, (New York : Daniel Fanshaw, 1821) 62.

pray," (Mark 14:38). "Watch ye therefore, and pray always," (Luke 21:36). Would it not be foolish to watch and pray, *sometimes?* The watchman is to be skilled at this watching and praying. He is to be held accountable to his work by God on behalf of others; their blood is on his hands if he mishandles them.

Like God, the watchman should not be confused about the word, or unable to communicate the word to the people boldly, faithfully and plainly. The watchman is never trying to get the message out of his head, but rather, he will be screwing it into the people's head, with boldness, clarity, precision and faithfulness whenever he speaks (do ministers do this today?).[13] The watchman must procure the most spiritual benefit he can in the shortest time he has among the people. He will not live forever; he does not know the end of his days. He will never preach enough sermons. George Whitefield, in the

---

[13] Church speakers, those in the pulpit of today's churches who do not belong there, are not true pastors, or real shepherds. They are a plague to Christendom, and continue to cripple contemporary believers. They are, for all preaching intents and purposes, *useless.* They only have a form of bible-talk or Christianese. If they are not fulfilling their commissioned duty to preach God's message in God's manner, they are useless, and they waste your time. You might think to yourself, "that seems rough, and we should not be so hard on them; ministers try, they are just men and even the best of men are just men." Useless is not my word, that's Christ's description. In his sermon to his newly ordained disciples, he says, "Ye are the salt of the earth, but if the salt has lost its savor, wherewith shall it be salted? It is henceforth good for nothing, but to be cast out, and to be trodden underfoot of men," (Matthew 5:13). Consider his words. Good for nothing. Cast out. Trodden underfoot; *i.e. useless.*

course of his life, preached 18,000 sermons which is *staggering*. Whitefield would tell you it was not enough.

Like God, the watchman can never be unskilled in the word. This does not mean that a watchman knows everything, or is limitless in his knowledge. Ezekiel did not by some "magic" suddenly know all things once God called him to be set as watchman. There is a great giving of the self to study and learning as a watchman; where Paul says "give thyself to reading," (1 Tim. 4:13), and where Ezekiel is to "eat" the book and "taste" it is sweet (Ezek. 2:9-3:3). And most commentators on this passage see Ezekiel not only directly getting information from the mouth of God, but from *all* that God had said, and all that was available to him in the covenant, and in the writings of those "preachers" before him. That meant any of the sacred Scriptures available; he knew their content in order to preach well. His preaching was not in a vacuum.[14]

It cannot be that a watchman is indifferent, boring, confused, unskilled or unwise in delivering the knowledge of God to the people. If they are, there is a great likelihood they are either in office prematurely, or they are not sent of God. Jeremiah was instructed, "And I will give you pastors according to mine heart, which

---

[14] In practicality, on this idea, John Calvin was first a scholar so he could be a good pastor. His faithfulness as a scholar, theologian, and pastor has set a biblical example of what it means to be a faithful servant of Christ. See his various biographies such as *A Life of John Calvin,* by Alister McGrath, and *Calvin, Geneva and the Reformation,* by Ronald S. Wallace.

shall feed you with knowledge and understanding," (Jer. 3:15). "I will give," God says. "I have set," God says, to the watchman, *you*, in this way. If God does not give a man to the ministry, then the church gets something else rather than what God gives. And that is a very dangerous place to be when people get what they want rather than who God gives. There is no more miserable place to be than a church without *God's* ordained watchman; one who preaches the word with knowledge and understanding which is something only Christ supplies in his grace. Churches are filled with ordained men, but God may not have sent them. The watchman must be responsible to know the word in order to understand it, in order to preach it, in order to apply it, and sound the alarm for God as a watchman for the people.

There is a great need of biblical watchmen in Christ's church. Isaiah said he lived among a people of unclean lips. He knew the people. He knew that they were sinful people. He dwelt among them. He was of their number. Watchmen must look diligently and meticulously, so that no one falls into sin. They are spiritual watchman, men of understanding, men of knowledge, men of beholding, where on his lips he must, "keep knowledge," (Mal. 2:7), that it might be given out as necessary to those who need it, even when those people don't know they need what he has. He is set by God and ordained of God to the watch. He does so even through the night, metaphorically speaking. "Watchman, what of the night? Watchman, what of the night? The watchman said, The morning cometh, and also the night: if ye will enquire, enquire ye: return, come," (Isa. 21:11-12). This means, the watchman is *always* on guard. He has much responsibility and must *always* be on guard. He does not sleep, metaphorically speaking. He cannot watch if he is sleeping. He cannot watch if he is not watching. What happens when watchmen sleep? Christ says, "But while men slept, his enemy came and sowed tares among the wheat, and went his way," (Matt. 13:25). If the watchman is sleeping, the devil takes advantage of the opportunity and brings into the lives of the people and the church those things, which if received, or heeded, will bring Christ's judgments...and whose fault is it? God requires his people to be free from those tools of the devil that will cause them to be wayward, (*i.e.* sinful). The watchman watches for such things and directs the people soundly to Christ in holiness.

God has labeled watchmen that do not watch with various names in Scripture: blind, ignorant, lazy, slothful, sleeping, *dumb dogs.* "His watchmen are blind: they are all ignorant, they are all dumb dogs, they cannot bark; sleeping, lying down, loving to slumber," (Isa. 56:10). Dogs are scavengers and of the most repudiated beasts in Scripture. They were not house pets. The use in Isaiah 56 is to set unfaithful watchmen as low as they can possibly be – dumb dogs. God separates himself from these kinds of people, for he did not send them; for *his* commissioned watchmen are very diligent.

41

God calls and ordains watchmen for the good of the church. "I have set thee a watchman unto the house of Israel." William Greenhill said, "Where watchmen are, dangers are supposed. There are church robbers abroad, that would rob it of the Scriptures, of ordinances, officers, of Christ, and of heaven itself."[15] The church is said to have wolves (heretics and false teachers) always trying to corrupt it (Ezek. 22:27; Hab. 1:8; Zeph. 3:3; Matt. 7:15, 10:16; Luke 10:3; Acts 20:29). Watchmen are very much needed; for they are not merely office bearers, position takers, but *watch*-men.

It is unfortunate that the vineyard of the Lord, even though it is tended, often brings up thorns and weeds. And little foxes, little things, that are out to destroy the vineyard are often found there. "Take us the foxes, the little foxes, that *spoil* the vines: for our vines have tender grapes," (Song 2:15). Watchmen behold these dangers; they discover and prevent danger in the church; and in its place minister Christ to the people. God has been exceedingly gracious to give the church the truth, all of it, once delivered to the saints (Jude 1). Watchmen are then given to preserve the church by the word, in the power of the Christ for the glory of God.

The duty of the watchman is to see the danger coming and blow the trumpet. Even that which just *appears* to be evil, that it might be avoided. "Abstain from all appearance of evil," (1 Thess. 5:22). How will they warn people if they do not see it? Evil destroys the

---

[15] Greenhill, Ibid, Ezekiel 29:7-9.

soul; it is murderous to growth in Christ (a violation of the sixth commandment). The watchman is to be on the lookout. When evil advances against the church in any form, or even its appearance, he blows the *shofar* (the horn of cautioning) and warns the people. Horns were symbols of power; Christ is the horn. Zechariah rightly applied this idea to the Christ, "And hath raised up an horn of salvation for us," (Luke 1:69). Christ is the horn they blow loudly, the one in whom brings safety and power. Such watchmen show the people under their charge the nature and danger of heresy, sin, evil, whether public or private, and they will not rest, they will not sleep, but instead stands vigilant at the watch, that they would cease to do evil, and learn to do good. And how often will the watchmen do this? Is he a watchman for a moment? Is he a watchman just on the Lord's Day? It is his *constant* vocation. This is why the preaching of the word and prayer are so important to him. Power (prayer) and guidance (preaching) are his tools, given by God.

Watchmen are for your good. These ministers, watchmen, come in the name and authority of God for *your* good. I hope you *receive* that fully. Many in the church today do not. They don't like watchman snooping into their *proverbial underwear drawer* and talking to them about their sins and their works and their duties, or *the lack thereof.* But, God says, "warn them from me," (Ezek. 33:7), which in turn shows that these watchmen have no fear of men, but a true fear of

God. Yet, you must be aware that God has sent them to you for your good; even though you might not like what they say to you now and again. But they are the voice of the Lord for you; the Lord's voice cries in the city to you. They do not, or should not speak on their own behalf, but for God. They are to be in touch with God and his word so much so that they speak what God wants them to speak when God desires them to speak it to you. They are here to tell you and warn you of both what sin does in ruining your relationship with Christ, and what grace can be found in the Savior that you need, and where those means are to gain the blessing, so that you see Christ as sweet and altogether lovely; not just lovely in the parts *you* like. They do it with circumstances and actions that apply to wicked courses that even have the appearance of evil. You are not to slight them for examining such things. They are required by God to do it. Many people hate this idea; many *ministers* hate this idea. It gives ministers the air of snoopiness in the lives of the people. The sinner does not want the minister snooping in on them. But they are watchman for you? They are required to be so, and they are negligent if they are not so; unless of course, you tell them that you don't want them to do that for you. In such cases, the watchmen has done his work, and you are merely neglecting the means of grace that God would use to guide you in the right, sanctifying way. William Greenhill, a very able watchman, said to his people, "Will you be so adverse to the work of the ministry? Can any sinner be so obstinate as not to consider, relent, and return, when God shall send one in his name to him, and the prophet shall say, "Sir, I come to you, and my life is at stake for you; if I do not tell you of your sins, I am a lost man. Give me leave therefore to deal plainly with you. You are covetous, unclean, proud, froward, ignorant, unbelieving, having a form of godliness without the power, and unless you take another course, and serve the living God otherwise than you do now, you will perish soul and body eternally; but if you will listen, I will show you the good and right way in Jesus Christ, the way everlasting, which will make you blessed for ever."[16] When the watchman comes to warn him, will the sinner rebuke him? Will the sinner not like the warning? When the watchman comes to a church congregation and counsels them by Scripture, should they listen, will they listen? It is deeply rooted in your human nature to rebel against it; but you have been given a new principle of vitality in Jesus Christ as one born again that desires to be changed by his power and guidance continually. How can you ever be angry with the work of the ministry in this way? When a watchman sent by God comes and deals in that way with you, do you really have a reason to hate his work, reject it, speak out against it, despise him coming so close to home at you? Should you not think, "Thank you for your counsel and exhortation, your admonitions, and by the grace of Christ and the power of the Spirit I will work to advance

---

[16] Greenhill, Ibid, 666.

what you have told me in expanding the kingdom of grace in my life for God's glory." God is very gracious to those that listen to the watchmen; our passage shows this; he is forgiving. For if they do not tell you, and if they do not counsel you, this passage in Ezekiel shows that their accounting to God of their stewardship will be horrible. "If thou do not speak to warn the wicked from his way, his blood will I require at thy hand," that is a scary verse for wayward ministers, for *negligent* ministers. But if you don't listen to the watchmen as he speaks for God, with God's word, you can bring judgment on yourselves; and displease your Savior.

If the watchmen brings you the word, and is a faithful watchman in that way, and if the watchman prays for you, and watches for you, and counsels you and preaches to you, and loves you, and is a faithful watchman in that way, if you do not listen to him, what does God say? "Whosoever heareth the sound of the trumpet, and taketh not warning, his blood shall be upon his own head." But, if you take the warning, take the instruction, receive the engrafted word with meekness, even as corrective or exhortative or preached in whatever way it comes from the watchman; safety lies in both the warning, and in the hearing as much as it does in the *doing* of whatever God says through his watchman; this is because the watchman is delivering Christ to you. And it is his job to be sure you stay on that right path, for you have not been called to the ministry as he has; and you have need of him if you profess allegiance to King Jesus as one of his people and his servants; he looks out for your soul as one standing in the watch, a minister that only God can make.

Chapter 2: The Watchman and Those He Watches

"So thou, O son of man, I have set thee a watchman unto the house of Israel; therefore thou shalt hear the word at my mouth, and warn them from me," (Ezek. 33:7).

Let me give you a reminder. So far, from the beginning of Ezekiel until chapter 33, Ezekiel had fulfilled what God was requiring of him as a watchman. He was set to call God's people to repentance in the context of his office as a watchman lest God's judgment reign down upon his house (which judgment comes in verse 21). If people do not listen to the watchman, their death is their own fault. Ezekiel, as a watchman, was without guilt if he sounds the trumpet, the alarm, even if no one reacts as they should. But Ezekiel would be very guilty if people perished as a result of his negligence in not sounding the alarm when the attack was present (verses 5–6).

The message of the trumpet, the metaphor of the trumpet, Ezekiel's "alarm" were warnings that God gave specifically to him and were of divine origin. "...therefore thou shalt hear the word at my mouth, and warn them from me," (Ezek. 33:7). He is God's spokesman, messenger, interpreter, his *watchman*. When God spoke to him, he would speak to the people, and he would deliver the message God had given him in its exactness and entirety and this would then fulfill what God set him to do.

Ezekiel is called literally to "watch." It is to take special notice of those things God requires. This has a direct relationship with who God is as holy, and what sin is as a transgression of his law, or lack of conformity to his law. Ezekiel, in watching the people for sin, is to attentively behold the object, to see if there is any danger approaching. If he sees anything to be done for the protection of the people, he is to blow the trumpet; the trumpet is Christ, the horn of salvation. He is to give them warning in order to stir up any actions that would enhance the church's well-being.

In all this, the Lord sets the watchman in his place. He is to tell the people, not by things he makes up, or what he thinks they want to hear, but by what God has already said; God's message for their good. "And warn them from me." Ezekiel as a watchman must not speak to the people in his own name, but *the voice of the Lord cries* in the mouth of the prophet.

With this considered, a watchmen has people to watch, and those watched are ordained by God to hear and do God's will under the watchman. Only God can make a watchman over his church, a minister of the Gospel. The watchman and minister are one and the same in this way. God alone is the Author of all offices in the church whether they are extraordinary or ordinary, and no man ought to come into any of them without a direct commission from God, called to church-work according to God's will. These watchmen are to be called to the office for a specific need in the church. Ministers are set apart and called primarily to watch and pray. Watching is set in two distinct areas, praying and preaching, and in those areas, there are many offshoots, some of which were discussed before; knowledge, preaching, boldness, faithfulness, *etc.* Ezekiel, as with all God's ministers, was set apart by God. Why? He was set as a watchman by God; and he does it through Jesus Christ, who is the Shepherd and Bishop of souls, for the good of his people. "For ye were as sheep going astray; but are now returned unto the Shepherd and Bishop of your souls," (1 Peter 2:25). God alone makes watchmen and sets them over his church. So, both scripturally and logically, if God sets a watchman *over his church*, there are, then, *those to be watched.* There are souls to watch over if there is a watchman. If the watchman is called and commissioned to watch, there are those to be watched over and in this they too have callings as well.

The two primary duties of the watchman are preaching and prayer. Ezekiel was instructed by God to give the precise word that he gave Ezekiel to the people, for power and guidance, prayer and preaching. As God's mouthpiece, the watchman's main occupation is prayer and the ministry of the word. The Apostles in fulfilling their commission as set watchmen over the church said, "But we will give ourselves continually to prayer, and to the ministry of the word," (Acts 6:4). In being watchmen, they sought out the best means to keep a watchful eye on the people, and the best means to minister as servants to them being appointed and set apart by God for the task of sounding the horn of salvation in Christ. The alarm would sound in their preaching, and power would be had for them and the church in their praying; they would be given power and guidance by the Lord. Acts 6 is where the first proto-type deacons were chosen that the watchmen might be exercised in being wise in giving themselves to that which causes them to watch well, set down in preaching and praying. Disseminating the word of God to the people, and prayers of all kinds; both for the people and themselves, is their primary task. Yet, quite simply, if there are preachers ordained to preach, then there are hearers ordained to hear. They have duties as well.

The two primary duties of those who hear, of covenanted believers who are "the watched" in the church (all those watched over), are *hearing and doing*. "Hearing and doing" hold a number of important aspects as it relates to the word of God; but we will only consider them generally. Consider first that Jesus said, "And he answered and said unto them, My mother and my brethren are these which hear the word of God, and do it," (Luke 8:21). James echoes this in, "But be ye doers of the word, and not hearers only, deceiving your own selves," (James 1:22). *Hearing and doing*.

HEARING – preaching and hearing are vitally linked. If there is a necessity on the watchman to watch, and in his watching there is preaching, by that office, to sound the alarm, there is a necessity on those who are watched to *listen* to the blowing of the horn. God had set and ordered his church, because of the work and merit of the chief elder Jesus Christ, to set down under-shepherds, elders, teachers, pastors, watchmen, and so if they are to watch, to preach, to instruct, to sound the alarm, to blow the trumpet, the people are to faithfully hear as much as the watchman is to faithfully preach. *Hearing* is part of the ordinance of preaching. "Faith commeth by hearing, and hearing by the word of God," (Romans 10:17); Paul's argument in Romans 10 is that hearing is done when the watchman heralds the good news of the Gospel of the horn of salvation. Hearing, in this way, is by the word of God, by God's institution of preaching by preachers, by the watchmen, so that those who are watched over can hear *what God says.* Wherever God has ordained people to attend his ordinances in worship or privately in the home, one is apt to find the communicated word there, which is a communication of the Christ. He is the living word; the horn of salvation. Every time, in any passage, in any part of Scripture, God speak, talks, demonstrates his will, sets down his commands, explains anything, gives an historical narrative, shows forth any revelation at all, it is always *the word communicated,* the Son, communicating and exegeting the Father to human beings who must, "hear ye him." Christ is the word, and the word is to be preached, and he is to be heard; he is the only horn of salvation that brings in the remedy to the spiritual forces of wickedness and sin.

Ezekiel 33 showed God setting the prophet as a *watchman* to preach his message, which came out of his prophet's human mouth, but was of divine origin. The people in this were obliged to hear; yes, it was a prophet speaking the physical words, but it was *God's voice* to them. If they did not hear, or did not want to hear, it was at no fault of the watchman if he had done what God required of him. If they listen, (if they heard), then they are respecting the watchman and his message, which they owe him as a representative of God and of Christ; this is implied in the hearing, for no one will ever hear a watchman who does not respect him. "Remember them which have the rule over you, who have spoken unto you the word of God: whose faith follow, considering the end of their conversation. Jesus Christ the same yesterday, and to day, and for ever," (Heb. 13:7-8). This is an amazing verse. *Who's faith follow*, what burden is placed on the watchmen, and what burden is placed on the watched to imitate Christ and follow *that* imitation? In this hearing and doing, those in the church are ruled, and this is not a bad thing but a very good thing. Christ, exalted in heaven, has dispensed his Spirit in such a way as to care for the watched, by watchmen, for in the watchman's words, if they preach God's words, and by the power of the Spirit, Christ is with them. He is with them in union, and he is with them in communion. Union in salvation and communion, or drawing near to them, is only possible when God communicates himself, and this occurs in the work and words of the watchman, by the words of the Scripture, and the people are further united to Christ by these words and power of the Spirit. They are ruled by those who speak the word of God on behalf of the One who is the same yesterday, today and forever; whose eternal word never changes. This is because they are all ruled by King Jesus, and this rule is in the manner in which King Jesus speaks by his word, in the mouths of the watchmen, if those watchmen are faithful. *The 1647 Westminster Confession of Faith*, says, "...officers in a single congregation, there ought to be one at the least, both to labour in the word and doctrine, and to rule," (Prov. 29:18; 1 Tim. 5:17; Heb. 13:7).[1]

Secondly, there is DOING – one of the great displays in the church by those watched over, who are born again, is that they obey those who rule over them, and obey God in his word; and this is the covenantal way of saying, they listen to the word of God responsibly preached, for watchmen, "watch for your souls, as they that must give an account, that they may do it with joy, and not with grief: for that is unprofitable for you," (Heb. 13:17). There is a great connection between this exhortation in Hebrews about rulers who rule, and those who are ruled in this way, by the word, under Jesus Christ, by way of giving account; *Hebrews* is expounding the idea of the watchman. The people know

---

[1] See the Form of Presbyterian church Government.

that watchmen must give an account of all they do; the question is whether they have ruled well or not. Have they watched well and looked over the souls of the people well? Is there blood on their hands as murders of souls, or are they as those who blow the trumpet and warn the people, to show a man his righteousness in the Christ? And the writer of Hebrews then applies this to *those* who *hear.* There is a hearing that is in accordance with godliness in this. Make note, those who are exhorted to hear, obey the word and the watchman by extension, "with joy and not with grief." Why does he say this? Because those watched over, often, having remaining sin, do not like to be ruled. They are often like wandering sheep, those who want to go into the wilderness of the world; they get caught in the thickets and briars of the world, and bleat for the Shepherd to come and rescue them. And the writer of Hebrews knows that they would make unimportant what they hear by the word if they do not esteem those they have been given by God over them, or do what is being taught. If these who are watched are not accepting of the watching of the watchmen, and if they resist their watchmen, it will be their grief, not simply sad, but to their eternal loss in many ways; which is the writer's point. They are not to have hard hearts as in the day of rebellion. Eternity is weighed in the balance at every word spoken by the faithful, bold, and plain watchman who preaches the Gospel.

But there is a catch in this: the watchman is one worthy of respect, and worthy of the office. Why would anyone want to submit to a tyrant, or some religious oppressor, or some negligent minister? Matthew Newcomen said, "The Lord promises to raise up unto his Church instruments fit for himself to use in this great work of restoring his Church and making it glorious, "I have set watchmen on thy walls, O Jerusalem," (verses 6-7).[2] Obedience should be rendered if watchmen speak God's words. The people are commanded to follow them, because it is God they are obeying. The Lord's voice cries to the people in the blowing of the trumpet of Christ. Christ is seen and ministered there as God's horn of salvation; the instrument of power. "Satan and his instruments being so very busy to deprave the church, that it is very necessary, that every one of Zion's Watchmen should give notice of the danger, and labor to fortify himself and the flock, against the devices of the common enemy for the good of the people," Michael Harrison said.[3] This obedience must be given with respect to the watchmen and their function. This is why the writer of Hebrews says, "submit yourselves" to those who rule over you, for that is a submission really, to the word of God they bring.

---

[2] Newcomen, Matthew, eBook, *The All-Seeing Unseen Eye of God, and Other Sermons*, (Coconut Creek, FL: Puritan Publications 2013) sermon 2, Jerusalem's Watchman.
[3] Harrison, Michael, eBook, *Christ's Righteousness Imputed, the Saint's Surest Plea for Eternal Life*, (Crossville, TN: Puritan Publications, 2016) To the Christian Reader.

Hearing the word profitably can never happen without submission; it is impossible. If the watched are not hearing by submission, giving due respect to the word and the watchmen of the word, who watch out for their souls, which is in reality due respect to the word itself, which is in reality due respect to the ordinance that God has setup, they can never become doers of the word; they will never respect what is being said. They will disrespect God. They are not submitted to the word; and to be "doers of it" would be impossible.

Yet, as a very important side note: do not place ministers on a pedestal; the word never teaches that; esteem them, but not immoderately (Acts 14:15). Certainly, the office has a level of elevation and certain qualities are attached to it, and the watchmen are esteemed for their work's sake. Those who are watched, look to the skill of the watchman for their good, for those skills come from the Spirit of God; for the Spirit is the one that makes them to differ (1 Cor. 12:4). They do not ascribe too much, or too little, to watchmen. It is the "Goldilocks Dilemma," having that which is just right, just in the right way. They do not despise them, or reject them, as the manner of some is if they do not like what they hear. But they are also not to esteem the minister as a principle author of divine truth, or someone elevated to unbiblical heights of immoderate praise. The watchman is a subordinate under Jesus Christ; he is a fellow believer. Yet, the watchman should be accounted more than an customary servant, for he has the burden

57

of bringing the word of God to the watched, that shows the people the way of salvation in Jesus Christ, as one among 1000, as it pertains to his office; it is only the burden of the office that elevates it. He is not a prognosticator, some predictor, or seer, or diviner, but rather a steward of God's word. He is a messenger, God's mouth to the people by preaching, and he is their mouth to God by praying for them. He has a very special standing in the church in that way. God speaks to him for them, then in his preaching he tells them what God has said, and then he speaks to God for them in his prayers. He stands in a special place before God, and ministers to God from the earth, and from the God of heaven to the people that dwell on earth. The Christian must take very special care that they do not fall out with their watchman, who the wisest God, has set and ordained to make them as rulers over them for their good. "Forsake not the Levite as long as thou livest upon the earth," (Deuteronomy 12:19). Francis Whiddon, a Westminster Divine, says of this, "do not desire such a teacher as you may rule him, but such as may rule you. Magistrates are chosen to govern the people, not the people to govern them. Likewise, you are not to command ministers, but to obey them."[4] The watched are to hear in respect and submission to the word of God by the preaching of those watchmen who have the rule

---

[4] Whiddon, Francis, eBook, *A Golden Topaz*, (Coconut Creek, FL: Puritan Publications, 2012) section under *The Preface*, <u>Preservatives</u>.

over them (by way of a weighty responsibility), to hear well, and not only hear but to do. God's case against his people in Ezekiel 33 was, "they sit before thee as my people, and they hear thy words, but they will not *do* them," (Ezek. 33:31). This was God's rebuke to the people after Ezekiel's preaching. Was this not Christ's rebuke?

> "And why call ye me, Lord, Lord, and do not the things which I say? Whosoever cometh to me, and heareth my sayings, and doeth them, I will shew you to whom he is like: He is like a man which built an house, and digged deep, and laid the foundation on a rock: and when the flood arose, the stream beat vehemently upon that house, and could not shake it: for it was founded upon a rock. But he that heareth, and doeth not, is like a man that without a foundation built an house upon the earth; against which the stream did beat vehemently, and immediately it fell; and the ruin of that house was great," (Luke 6:46-49).

It is interesting that the Lord uses the word, "ruin" for the one that is not a *doer* of the word.

What happens when those who are watched in the church do not do what they hear? Know, first, that those who are lost will *always* reject the word of God, if not superficially, yet, deeply and with hatred. Why? "Because the carnal mind is enmity against God: for it is not subject to the law of God, neither indeed can be," (Rom. 8:7). Doers of the word are blessed in what they do before God, where mere professors who hear and do not do, are self-deceived, and they satisfy themselves with a dead faith that does not work; (I do not want to deal with that here as I have done in other works.[5]) But, as it pertains to the godly, what is the reason why believers, those who have a watchman over their souls in Christ, do not do what the word says? They do not make further strides in religion, sometimes make little use or growth from the preached word, and why is not more growth seen in the church? It is because they only hear the word and do not *do* the word, for the word of God makes no lasting impression on them after they hear it; this was Christ's rebuke to his disciples.[6] This is Christ's point; it is God's point in Ezekiel even though they had a watchman over them. It is God's very case against them. The Lord Jesus and the Apostle James both contrast the mere hearer, and the practical student of Scripture against one another. This is really what Ezekiel 33 is saying about hearers. The way the people of a church esteem the word of God or not will show in their growth or their deficiency. They will be as religious

---

[5] See my work, *Joseph's Resolve and the Unreasonableness of Sinning Against God.*

[6] Make note that one of the most important times, of seeing whether or not the word of God *impresses* people (has impressed itself on them), is right after the church service ends. What people will talk about will determine what has impressed them or not.

as they were a year ago, as they are today with no growth.

Many churches in the world see the words of the watchman like a word from a brother; where they are happy when one *shares* something with them, but not so happy when they are *preached* to. I think many watchmen, as well as those watched, think about it in this way. They do not esteem the word as they ought; they look at it from a human perspective and something that is less than what it ought to be, and they do not really believe it is God speaking directly to them. Is it not, "the Lord's voice [crying] in the city?" (Micah 6:9). Yes, it is the prophet Micah's *voice* crying out in preaching in Micah 6:9, but is it not *the Lord's voice* crying in the city? Is it not the Lord's voice crying in the church? John Brinsley said it this way about those who do not want to *do* the word, "they come to hear the Word, [and] they look on it with a squinted eye."[7] But isn't Peter's exhortation about this, "to desire the sincere milk of the Word," (1 Peter 2:2), the remedy of the horn of salvation blown, to desire milk that is pure to satisfy *that they may grow thereby?* Sincere hearts will always desire after sincere milk; and they look for nourishment from Jesus Christ and his word, for his sheep hear his voice; and they find the Lord's voice in the mouth of the

---

[7] Brinsley, John, eBook, *The Preacher's Charge and People's Duty*, (Crossville, TN: Puritan Publications, 2016), Part 7: Hearing the Word Preached.

preacher, the one watching over their souls; and are *happy* for it.

In this preaching, the watchman presents God's Christ both to the ears and hearts of the hearers, for watchmen draw Christ "out" of Scripture, "...to crucify him before them," (Gal. 3:1). They must receive him, hear the message, the horn of salvation, and take in the sweetness of the Christ, in the manner in which God instructs from his word; and this can pertain to all kinds of Scriptural directions. The watched must hear the word and do the word in the same liveliness and strength that the preacher preaches the word; they expect a good preacher, don't they? Preachers expect good Christians too. They are to hear the word and do it with earnestness, and with diligence; which is the way the preacher should preach in earnestness and diligence, boldly, faithfully and clearly.[8] If preachers are required to preach well, hearers are required to hear well; this they do with joy and not with grief, for that would be unprofitable for them.

There is a great need of earnestness in stirring up the heart to *do* the word if it will have successful effects for them in a church. Christians have a natural sin nature that dislikes to do the word; it is why people sin; it is why Christians still sin (Romans 7). Christians have this as remaining sin. What they want to do, they do not do... There are so many distractions that pull Christians off

---

[8] If preachers are required to be vibrant, lively, faithful, bold preachers, equally, the Christians hearing ought to be same.

the path, where sin takes hold and leads them into the way or that way. They do not want to climb the hill of difficulty. They would rather take the way that is far more easy on their feet, as Christian talked Hopeful into in Bunyan's *Pilgrim's Progress*; let's take the easy road, the easier path; this led them straight to doubting castle. Christians are often so used to living in a dull manner, often weary, and they do this privately many times, without ever seeking guidance, that they have little to no power to be sensitive to the Spirit ministered to them in the word. Did not Eutychus fall from the window at Paul's sermon in Acts 10:9? There is a sermon somewhere in there to get a good night's sleep the night before in preparation for the day in which the watched hear the watchmen and the word of the Lord. It cannot be that the watched have their bodies in the place, but their hearts and minds are somewhere else. What good would that do? In such works the Apostle Paul says to those being watched by watchman, "Continue in prayer, and watch in the same," (Col. 4:2). "What," the watched ask, "I have to watch too?" Oh yes, they are watched over, and yet, they too must "hear and do," "watch and pray." Jesus certainly instructed his ministers in this, watch and pray, but then he says, "And what I say unto you I say unto all, watch," (Mark 13:37). The watched are loaded not only with being submissive under the word of the watchmen themselves, but they too are to watch, and in this they are hearers and doers of the word.

You must see in this, first, that there is the privilege of a watchman to a church. Some churches have no watchman. Some churches have poor watchman. Some churches have church speakers, instead of preachers. Some churches have false shepherds and wolves, even if they seem very nice and shake people's hands, and have a jolly disposition. How many churches have you ever been in where the minister would sit down with you and talk to you about your personal lives, and your personal sanctification in some common manner, and that regularly? Where did a minister ever sit with you and say, "Tell me about the nature of your sin that so easily besets you in actual sins you commit," and then they give you a biblical strategy to overcome them from the Bible? I don't believe I have ever, in all my years, been in a church where the watchman was actually watching out for me in that way; how terrible! How many sins could have been avoided if they did?

As poorly as Richard Baxter may have been a very terrible theologian on some important doctrines, the work he did as a watchman in the town of Kidderminster, turned it from being a reprobate place of lewdness and drunkenness, to him walking down the streets on the Lord's Day to hear the people all singing psalms from their houses; this did not only happen by preaching from the pulpit, but by counseling with the people and directing them personally. Why are there no ripples across the United States of massive revivals, with so many churches? The reason is that biblical watchmen, who blow the horn and sound the alarm, are *scarce*.

And you reader, consider it, when has a minister sat down with you and strategized for the good of your soul, and life, to help minister to you in being more Christlike, to discuss combat for the Kingdom and the King, and your pressing into the kingdom? Where have they ever fulfilled their watching over you in the way they ought, so that you can live in the manner you desire to please Jesus? Is there blood on their hands whom you have sat under in times past? Isaiah knew those he was commissioned to preach to. "I dwell amongst a people of unclean lips." Where have such ministers helped you in situations you would rather have them not see, where that problem, in and of itself argues their need for you? Do you have a place where sin steals your heart away from Jesus; what is the remedy for it? The first part of the remedy is that Christ has given watchmen over the church for our good. Do you seek them out?

The privilege of the watchmen over our souls is a privilege of the local body; it is a privilege of church membership. When Paul was converted, the first order of business was to join the church. Why? because there are no, "Lone Ranger Christians." "And when Saul was come to Jerusalem, he assayed to join himself to the disciples," (Acts 9:26). First order of business after his conversion was to get under the watchmen. But interestingly, the watchmen there *would not let him* be a member until Paul showed himself to be a Christian.

The watchmen were watching him. The church at Jerusalem exercised this under the apostles. The privileges of the watchman are not primarily for the vagabond who wanders in off the street. Pastoral oversight is a privilege of those who are members of a visible community of believers and their children, as the *1647 Westminster Confession of Faith* explains.[9] Watchmen are given for covenanters – those who make a public profession based on faith and like-mindedness in doctrinal matters concerning unity in a local body which they are part of; in which they join, along with their household, to the glory of Jesus Christ and his saving work. Many people do not like *that* idea – that they must "join". In fact, they do not want pastoral oversight at all; they do not want to be submissive or ruled. They are content to come to hear the word each week in a church, take communion if it is offered, and go home, and decide for themselves what they will do and believe and what they won't; with no watchman to call them into account. It is a very perilous time where a person in their home professes to be a Christian yet will not join with others publicly in that profession as a covenanter. "*Perilous* you say?" Yes, very much so. Even seen prophetically in Jeremiah 4:2, "And you shall swear, 'The LORD lives,' In truth, in judgment, and in righteousness; The nations shall bless themselves in Him, And in Him they shall glory.'" Even in prophecy, in

---

[9] See both the *Sum of Saving Knowledge* and the *Directory for Private Worship.*

Gospel times, vowing is to take place as commanded by God, "you shall swear." Instead, they say, "I don't want to do that." Well, then, if the watchman pays you no mind and gives you no help, no spiritual guidance, *don't complain;* and if he does not look out for your soul, then know, you are on your own; the means God has given you, you are rejecting. If all things for you come to an eternal loss, don't complain about it. If you are not fulfilling God's requirement of a professing Christian, you act as a rebel, which actually contributes to the perilous sins of the day. You might be thinking, "There you go again with this idea of it being "perilous days." How is this so?" Paul said that. He taught specifically on it in two passages using the word *perilous* itself. "This know also, that in the last days perilous times shall come," (2 Tim. 3:1). In this passage he said such people are, "without natural affection, trucebreakers," (2 Tim. 3:3). These are covenant breakers, not keepers; those who refuse to enter into covenant is literally his use of the terms here and in Romans 1. They might be hearers but they are not *really* hearers for they are not submitted to the watchmen over them and they are not really doers of the word. Such people are truce breakers who have no watchman; perilous times indeed are upon them.

Who do you vow to when you join the church? You vow to Christ, through under-shepherds, with the people, "Let the elders who rule well be counted worthy of double honor, especially those who labor in the word and doctrine," (1 Tim. 5:17). "...they shall vow a vow unto the LORD, and perform it," (Isa. 19:21). You submit to the elders of the church who govern you; you are a governed people if you are Christian people; and you are happy to do so if the elder is an elder and a deacon is a deacon as God intends. "And we urge you, brethren, to recognize those who labor among you, and are over you in the Lord and admonish you, and to esteem them very highly in love for their work's sake," (1 Thess. 5:12-13). You should have a very high esteem for their work; but never immoderately, never placing them on a pedestal; you are to remember them, and give heed to their words. "Remember those who rule over you, who have spoken the word of God to you, whose faith follow, considering the outcome of their conduct," (Heb. 13:7). These elders, these watchmen, watch out for your souls and rule over you; and as they do so following Christ, who should be demonstrating a holy conduct before you, so imitate them. "Obey those who rule over you, and be submissive, for they watch out for your souls, as those who must give account. Let them do so with joy and not with grief, for that would be unprofitable for you," (Heb. 13:17); again, explaining Ezekiel 33.

Today in our counter culture, people don't like that word obey; *obey them.* But the church is not to be run with some kind of gym-membership mentality. One comes in, tries things out for some thirty days, or 30 years, and then decides they don't want to work out anymore so they leave. This is why many professing Christians do not want to join a church – it is because they do not want to be responsible to that church; to the watchman or the people. They are *mere professors* in this. They do not want to be subject to godly authority, they do not want a watchman over them, who can tell them what they can and cannot do before the Lord as the Scriptures give God's preachers leave; they might want to hear, but they want to decide what to do or not do.

As Christians we are all governed in Christ's church, have oversight in his church, have privileges in his church, and are to be submissive in his church to the elders as covenanted members who have vowed to do so publicly. You are bound by this, to both hear and obey the word, which is the voice of Christ. When the watchman speaks to us, we should think God is speaking if they are preaching the word boldly, plainly and faithfully. And that is no small matter to God in light of his glory and for our good. You "take a stand" (as with Josiah in his reformation) in that covenant by submission to the rule of God and his watchmen before the eyes and ears of others (2 Kings 23:2-4). Otherwise, without this, there is no need for governing of any kind in the church. As many churches are, and the way they act, they are just big bible studies. But in doing that, you would in fact reject God's constituted means of grace, the work of Christ and the power of the Spirit in the work of the watchman in the church.[10] If governing souls, *taking heed to them*, is something the Lord

---

[10] See my work *5 Marks of a Biblical Church*, for a full discussion of church membership.

requires of his watchmen, then the opposite to "governing souls" is biblically unsound. It would be sinful – a perilous sin – if those watched do not want to be watched, where Paul says about such, that they are truce-breakers, "...knowing the righteous judgment of God, that those who practice such things are deserving of death," (Rom. 1:32). "...having a form of godliness but denying its power. And from such people turn away!" (2 Tim. 3:5). Church discipline itself is a privilege of membership in the church in this very regard. Why a privilege? It is for a Christian's good because it is instituted by Christ himself, Christ being in their midst when the two or three are gathered for such purposes; which is the direct context of that statement in Matthew 16 and 18. Jesus *died* for the church, and very much cares that it is governed and watched over in a manner of godliness that stands in accordance with his dying for it, and his present intercession for his people. Christ never says that his church is to be filled with corruption; he did not die for it to remain corrupted. It is to be discernably purged of it; and church discipline is a help in this when it is warranted, but one cannot be excommunicated from nothing unless he is a member of something.

We are to be faithfully watched over, which is a great privilege in Christ's church. We are to hear their words and do their words as they are in accordance with godliness for our good. Such preservation of our souls in the church is for edification: discipline in this way is either preventative or corrective; did you know that every time the watchman preaches, it is an act of church discipline? It keeps us as Christians from straying from Christ and sinning against his body and blood, which is preventative church discipline. Anything that challenges and corrects us from a known sin is corrective church discipline (both of which are bound up in the preaching of the word and the watching of the watchman. But this can never happen for our good without submission to the word, in hearing and doing, and in this way esteeming the words of the watchman, as those who are watched over.

There are privileges to membership in the church that we do not get without it. You are spiritually watched over by Jesus Christ, through his watchmen. What a gracious thing Christ does in this way. That is why Saul, later Paul, wanted to join the church. "Join," to glue himself to them; to fasten and cleave to them. Christians are to be glued to it, and what is it but oversight under the watchmen as those watched. "Obey those who rule over you," (Heb. 13:17). "Obey," be persuaded and to comply, and the phrase "be submissive" is better translated as "do not resist them." The watchmen of the church are not instructed by God to do this watching for everyone in the world, but only for those in the church, those special particular people, those they are to watch over in a geographic location. And it is the church's privilege to have one, and as the Lord wills, maybe more than one.

There are churches all over the world who have lecterns with men, but they are *not* watchmen. There are churches all over the world who have leaders, but they are *not* watchmen. There are churches all over the world filled with administrators, *infotainment church speakers*, but they are *not* watchmen. How can the watched hear if the watchmen are not watching?

In considering our own church, the one I preach in weekly, and think, what is it that God would look to the faithful here in this place to have not one, but, Lord willing, two, three, four, or more watchmen, in this place? I think about the people of my church who are highly esteemed indeed by Jesus Christ to have elders in this way, according to his gracious will: they are the, "beloved of God, called to be saints," (Rom. 1:7). What a great calling they have in this, and what a privilege to have one, two, three or five elders!

Secondly, your preparation in this "hearing" is as important as the watchman's preparation for sermonizing, or warning. If you are watched over, and the primary duty of the watchman is to deliver the word he has prayed about and studiously (meticulously) set down to preach to you, then you must take seriously the work of hearing the word that you will be able to *do* the word. If you are going to sanctify God's name in hearing the word, you must first understand that such hearing and doing *is worship*.[11] As one "watched over," you

---

[11] See Puritan Publication's volume by Jeremiah Burroughs, *Gospel Worship.*

profess your dependence on God for knowing his mind; he has instructed you as to his ordinances, and the watchmen preaches, which is the height of the act of worship as God speaks, and as you hear. He has so ordered preaching as to be a benefit for you, and that which he most loves in the midst of Zion. This argues greatly for your attentiveness and preparation to hear the word in order to do it well.

In hearing the word, there must be a preparation. Briefly, remember just two things. When you hear the word, hear it as the word of God. "...when ye received the word of God which ye heard of us, ye received it not as the word of men, but as it is in truth, the word of God, which effectually worketh also in you that believe," (1 Thess. 2:13). And this was the point in my work, *The Lord's Voice Cries in the City*, on Micah 6:9. It was Micah's voice preaching, yes, but it was the *Lord's voice* if Micah preached *God's word*.

And also, secondly, you hear the word of the watchman as God's good ordinance for your growth in Christ. Really, this is linked to guidance, and power. It is to see Christ more clearly, which in turn, causes you to grow closer to him.[12] Your heart is ploughed up, sin is pointed out, righteousness is demonstrated, and Christ crucified is preached to you that you might take hold of him by faith and grow thereby in godliness. In the *Chronicles of Narnia*, Edmund had sinned in Narnia, by

---

[12] I would direct you more fully to my work, *Seeing Christ Clearly*, in that way, which gives a full discussion of that.

co-mingling with worldly things, he touched and took and pocketed some treasure, and was turned into a dragon. It was unpleasant to be a boy *and then* a dragon. Aslan (the Christ figure in the books) had to use his sharp claws and physically rip the scales from his flesh to turn him back into boy. Scale-ripping can be hard, but worth it in the end. Such scale-ripping is by the word, it is done by the preaching of the watchman. In this you are resolved to hear well that you do well that all the truths delivered in the blowing of the horn by the watchman, you take for the truth of the most high God to see Christ clearly and to be conformed to his image. You submit with joy and not with grief to those instructions, and you come to know the salvation and eternal life of the Christ more; you know it to be a benefit for you. In this you sincerely desire the pure milk of the word, for you, week by week, cultivate a great desire to hear the watchman and discern his power of watching. And if such a desire is cultivated, you will, through prayer, ready yourself to hear the voice of the Shepherd to the sheep.

And yet, secondly, there must be a doing. Your soul has a certain behavior that occurs when you hear well and that is to do well. You give careful attention to the word. You pray for your heart to be opened to receive whatever God will show you. You then carefully apply that word to your life, mixing it with faith in Christ, and looking for the Spirit to help you walk victoriously in the

Lord. A hearing well will yield you to doing well as you walk victoriously in the power of the Spirit.

Let me also place upon your shoulders another weight, which is not a burden, but a privilege. Did you know that you personally, as members of Christ's church in a geographic location, participate in electing ministers to the church? The subject of the appointment of watchmen to watch over you, the ordinary and outward calling of a minister has two parts — election and ordination. Election is where you choose out a person, or persons, most able to the office that is providentially needed, and by your consent to whom the person or persons be appointed. "No man is to be ordained a minister for a particular congregation, if they of that congregation can shew just cause of exception against him," the *1647 Westminster Confession of Faith* says.[13] No one can "lord" themselves over you. God must send them, and God has certain means of sending them. You must be prepared to receive them if the Lord is sending them. No one can come into the church to be a watchman contrary to the will of the congregation to whom they are looking to be appointed, without their voice; you are to watch the watchman in this light. Such a watchmen set over you, must be duly qualified, both for life and ministerial abilities, according to the rules of the apostle; and tested as such in both doctrine and preaching. We saw that in 1 Tim. 3:2-6 and Tit. 1:5-9. He is to be examined and approved by those by whom he is

---

[13] See the Form of Presbyterian Church Government on *Ordination*.

to be ordained (1 Tim. 3:7, 10; 5:22; 1 Tim. 3:2; Tit. 1:7); he is to be seen by you, and preach and teach a certain number of times before you and then you decide; to see his watchful abilities exercised in your midst, but keep in mind; I'm oversimplifying it. But you have, then, a very great duty to consider such things if God so wills it; prayerfully so. For that person to be ordained as a watchman receives a ministerial charge to watch over you, and you agree to it; for he watches out for your never dying soul; he will be responsible to you and you to him in your preparation and hearing and doing of what he instructs you from the word (Acts 14:23; 20:17, 28; Titus 1:5). He watches, over the watched, that he might preach and teach and pray, that he might bring God's message, that those ordained to hear would hear, do, and grow into the full stature of Jesus Christ, and that they would in fact, then, have a ministry in the family, the church, and the world.

Chapter 3:
The Faithfulness of the Watchman

"So thou, O son of man, I have set thee a watchman unto the house of Israel; therefore thou shalt hear the word at my mouth, and warn them from me," (Ezek. 33:7).

As a manner of remembrance, Ezekiel was God's watchman. He was set to call God's people to repentance in the context of his office as a watchman lest God's judgment reign down upon his house (which judgment comes in verse 21). If people do not listen to the watchman, their death is their own fault. Ezekiel as a watchman was without guilt if he sounds the trumpet, the alarm, even if no one reacts as they should. But Ezekiel would be very guilty if people perished as a result of his negligence in not sounding the alarm when the attack was present (verses 5–6). He is the one who "observes, and fixes the eyes to see and understand its object." This is to take special notice of something. The watchman warns, "if when he seeth the sword come upon the laud," *etc.* He is to attentively behold the object, to see if there is any danger approaching. If he sees anything to be done for the protection of the people, is to blow the trumpet. He is to give them warning in order to stir up any actions that would enhance the church's well-being. The Lord sets this watchman in his place. He is to know the word, alarm sinners of the word, and help them to see what sin and righteousness are, what punishments or blessings might come, what God's wrath is or his divine favor in his covenant, and such. He is to preach and pray, to give direction and power by the Holy Spirit on behalf of Christ.

Also, as there is a watchman, so there are the watched. The people hear God's voice crying in the preaching of the word. They hear and do what God has spoken. They hear the watchman preaching as the voice of the Lord cries in the mouth of the watchman.

Watchmen discharge their office by directing to and exalting Jesus Christ, which is the work of the Gospel ministry, and the watched receive this Christ with peace, hope and joy.

All things in ministry are directed to exalt the Christ. How does the watchman exalt the Christ? Exalting Christ is seen in two ways. There is the sight of his excellency. That the watchman makes Christ to the watched excellent in his person and work. Such an idea covers a great vast array of biblical truth. Secondly, there is also the sense of his benefits. That the watchman makes the communicative benefits of Christ's person and work accessible to those watched. It is one thing to theologically set forth Christ as *excellent* in all his ways and works, but quite another thing to make the excellency of Christ *tangible* to the sinner, experiential; that they *experience* forgiveness, sanctification, etc., which is the work of the Holy Spirit on the soul. But the means by which the Spirit will work on the soul, is through "ordained means" such as the watchman. The watchman is given this task by skilled preaching of the word of God, which is used by the Spirit to conform people to Christ.

It would be an important question to ask, "What is the goal and end of preaching the Gospel?" Is it to save sinners? No. Is it to sanctify Christians? No. The goal and end of preaching by the watchman is to exalt Christ and glorify the living God; the supremacy of God in preaching is the first end. If sinners are saved, and Christians sanctified, these are happy *consequences* of preaching, what would be called *a subordinate end* of preaching because the supremacy of God in preaching is found in glorifying Christ and exalting God as its main aim. God seeks to communicate himself to his creatures in a certain way. He said, "...therefore thou shalt hear the word at my mouth" (Ezek. 33:7). God will glorify himself in that communication. "Then shall they know that I am the LORD," (Ezek. 33:29). The goal of the watchman, the herald, the goal of redemptive preaching, is a declaration, a show, a display of God and Christ's glory. Shout the Gospel loudly: YOUR GOD REIGNS! (Isaiah 52:7), "How beautiful upon the mountains are the feet of him who brings good news, who proclaims peace, who brings glad tidings of good things, who proclaims salvation, who says to Zion, "Your God reigns!"" He reigns supreme in all things. The very reason God created the world was for his own glory, and he does all things for his glory. The enthronement of God preached before the people, God reigning, is the heart of the salvation message. It is the *what* of the Gospel.[1] So see Christ enthroned, to see the glory of God, is the heart-desire of every saint. "And he said, I beseech thee, shew me thy glory," (Exod. 33:18). This is really a request to see the incarnation of God, to see God. "Behold, the LORD our God hath shewed us his glory and his greatness, and we have heard his voice out of the midst of the fire: we have seen this day that God doth talk with man, and he liveth," (Deut. 5:24). Where is the glory of God seen? "And the Word was made flesh, and dwelt among us, (and we beheld his glory, the glory as of the only begotten of the Father,) full of grace and truth," (John 1:14). In the incarnation of the horn of salvation, Jesus Christ, is the full glory of God seen and experienced. How God does this, is through Christ fulfilling the reign of God in the world, and the reign of God in the hearts of sinners converted by his Gospel. Psalm 29:10 says, "The LORD sat enthroned at the Flood, And the LORD sits as King forever." Psalm 22:3 says, "But You are holy, Enthroned in the praises of Israel." And yet, by Spirit-power, God aims to exalt himself and accomplish his purposes in and through the watchman and for the watched, for his bride, for his church, in those means. This watchman, then, should have God's

---

[1] See my work, *The Kingdom of Heaven is Upon You*, for a full orbed view of the preaching of the Kingdom. And also, *The Five Principles of the Gospel*, for a complete view of what Paul meant in quoting Isaiah on the "beautiful feet" of preachers who preach the Gospel.

intentions in mind, never his own. Isaiah 55:11 says quite emphatically, "So shall My word be that goes forth from My mouth; It shall not return to Me void, but it shall accomplish what I please, and it shall prosper in the thing for which I sent it." What is that *thing?* The *thing* is that God reigns through his Christ. This is what is foremost on the mind of the watchman! God's singular aim is not to exalt the preacher, nor to make people like the preacher, or to placate himself, or pacify the people. It is to bring Christ glory and announce his message of supreme rule as King Jesus and Savior. This is why God commissions watchman.

The commission of the watchman is set in being God's mouthpiece, and watching on behalf of those God desires to rule and reign by the power of his exalted Son. Such a watchman is charged by God in the supremacy of God in preaching. Watchmen are given a charge, a commission by God himself to a particular office in his church to minister Jesus Christ. It is a commission where the sender is God, and the one commissioned is the herald of the Christ; and what a special place it is for the watched to hear! The ones sent by God are watchmen to watch for the good of the church; heralds to proclaim his glory, and the watched are ordained to hear. Jesus even sends watchmen forth amidst difficulty in their occupation and commission, when he says, "I send you forth as lambs among wolves," (Luke 10:3). In the midst of those that will hate them in the world, Jesus sends them by his command and for his glory.

The watchman is commissioned in light of the fall, and all things are in reference to the difficulty of the fall. They are lambs, amidst wolves, but sent by the power of the Christ which is protective in whatever way God so deems for their good; which in itself shows forth the Shepherd imagery over his sheep. "So thou, O son of man, I have set thee a watchman unto the house of Israel;" (Ezek. 33:7); what can wolves really do if the power of Christ, the Shepherd, is with the lamb? In light of being a fallen son of man, one that is directly related to the fall of Adam, one that is a descendant of such, Ezekiel has been set a watchman, not over humanity, but over the house of Israel, the church. It is a particular group of people in a geographic location. He is to minister there, to watch those people, in that place. He is to show his people the promise of the Christ, whether 12 people, or 1200.

The minister has a particular commission, a particular post, and must be sure he is set over that post with the clear vision of God. He sees his post in light of the fall. He is connected to the people he has charge over in light of the fall. He is a watchman for the very purpose of fighting and reversing the effects of the fall on the people of the church through exalting the Christ and demonstrating the word and all its glory for God.

God is very concerned first with his glory, and second with his people. He is so concerned that he commissions faithful watchmen to watch over and pray for his church; and he is so serious about that, that God says if the watchman does not bring his message in his way and his ministry in his way, he will require the people's blood on the watchman's account. Such a commission is given by God but recognized by the watchman being sent; and the watchman agrees to do it. All watchmen say, as Isaiah said, "Here am I, send me."

There are certain evidences of a commission that must be noticed. Does Ezekiel have a desire for the work as a prophet of God? Such a desire is necessary. "This is a true saying, If a man desire the office of a bishop, he desireth a good work," (1 Tim. 3:1). It is a permeant desire, to make him willing to take the office and work of a minister for life. There must be a deep sense of personal weakness and unworthiness in it. Paul said, "Who is sufficient for these things?" (2 Cor. 2:16); no one apart from God's power is sufficient for anything. There must be some degree of confidence that God will enable the minister to do his work. "And such trust have we through Christ to God-ward: not that we are sufficient of ourselves to think any thing as of ourselves, but our sufficiency is of God, who also hath made us able ministers of the New Testament," (2 Cor. 3:4-6).

There also must be a high estimation of the office itself before God. A desire for the work overlaps on this; it even flows into the minds of those watched. There must be, as William Plumer says, "in the church itself, a consent of the proper authorities."[2] "...look ye out among you seven men of honest report, full of the Holy Ghost and wisdom, whom ye may appoint over this business," (Acts 6:1-6). Plumer continues, "From this portion of Scripture it is exceedingly evident, that the concurrence of the people's election, and of the ordaining authority's approbation, is necessary to the validity of the commission of even a deacon, whose office extends only to the temporalities of the Church. Much more, then, have the people a right to choose the man who is to be their counselor, and teacher, and guide."[3] Watchman minister Jesus Christ first for the glory of God, and then for the good of those watched over (Isaiah did that, he saw the Christ, and desired to be sent). What would the watchman do in his ministry? To demonstrate how God forgives, how Christ pardons, (Exod. 34:9), to spare, (Neh. 13:22), to cover, (Psalm 32:2), to blot out, (Isa. 43:25), to mention no sin, (Ezek. 33:16), not to lay sin to one's charge, (Acts 7:60), not to impute sin, (Rom. 4:8), to be merciful, and not to remember sin any more, (Heb. 8:12), for the good of people and their comfort. The church looks to pray to Christ for the glorification of his mercy and power in them, which is what the minister prays for and preaches about. There a watchman can declare a man his righteousness (Job 33) and the pardoning of man's sins against God, will be as if one

---

[2] Plumer, William, eBook, *The Bible's Teaching on the Call to the Ministry*, (Crossville, TN: Puritan Publications, 2017), section Evidences of a Call to the Ministry.
[3] Ibid.

should cross out a debt from an accounting book, Psalm 32:1, "Whose sins are forgiven." In Hebrew this means to take away, having reference to Christ, who bare and "took away the sins of the world," (John 1:29). "None of his sins that he hath committed shall be mentioned unto him," (Ezek. 33:16). This is where the watchman goes for the good of the people that God may declare them justified in their sight, on account of Jesus Christ and his glory. He, "Remembreth them no more," (Heb. 8:12).

Are watchmen, then, in glorifying God's mercy in Christ and extending that mercy to sinners to turn and live and grow and be vessels of honor, to be faithful? "But if the watchman see the sword come, and blow not the trumpet, and the people be not warned..." It is true, all those who have on "watchmen shoes" do not necessarily fill those whose as they ought, nor does it mean they are necessarily faithful. Some are asleep at their post, some are careless at their post, some men ought not even to be at such a post having appointed themselves to the task; such men whose real *desire* is merely to go with the flow of the world and the trendiness of the church. Some watchman are blind watchmen, shepherds that do not feed their flock, "salt without its saltiness," Jesus said to his disciples. They may stand in a pulpit, but they have no virtue in their work. They have nothing of Christ to give the people so that the watched may suck virtue from Christ in spiritual power and direction. They wouldn't even know how to direct Christians to do that! They might even be in fact heretical watchmen who poison their people; preachers of old called such false preachers "murderers of souls" taken from this passage in Ezekiel 33.

There are watchmen who preach only general truths, but without application to the flock, never giving them any practicality in their walk, because they do not know their flock and their needs. Thomas Hodges, a Westminster Divine, said, "Application is the salt and the soul of a sermon. Such preachers are like sword fencers, that make a great flourish, but never strike to purpose."[4] I've had people personally tell me, "I liked the first part of the sermon, but hated the last 15 minutes." The last 5 minutes is where the *application* is found. Watchmen are keen to apply what they know to be true about God; *i.e.* the wisdom that comes from the knowledge of Scripture.

Look at what Ezekiel is to preach. He was given very specific soul-searching truths to declare to sinners and to the church God's message to glorify God and to bring sinners into a right relationship with God. Turn and live; repent, live righteously, follow God, honor the Lord; very practical truths indeed. There are watchmen that have a desire to teach others, but in their actions, in their ministry, they have no virtue in themselves. They might preach fairly well, but live terribly. The metaphor of a watchman for the minister proves that the minister

---

[4] Hodges, Thomas, eBook, *The Necessity, Duty and Dignity of Gospel Ministers*, (Crossville, TN: Puritan Publications, 2017) section, The Duty of Ministers.

ought to admonish their flocks of enemies, warn them of impending disaster, and what steps they may take to be vigilant before God, and in these current days, vigilant in Jesus Christ as good soldiers to glorify the Christ even amidst all the affliction in the world, or being unpopular. If the minister has no virtue in himself, and is not watching over his own life (piety) and the life of his family, how shall he watch over the church? In bible college and seminary, I cannot tell you any time, when any teacher, any teaching ministers or professors, taught about the nature and function of family worship or personal private worship. *Not one time.* This is beyond tragic in our day.

Watchmen are skilled in hearing God and discerning God's intended message for those he watches over. "...therefore thou shalt hear the word at my mouth," (Ezek. 33:7). The watchman is to minister Jesus Christ in all his ways and teach the whole counsel of God. If the watchman does not know the word, is not skilled in the word, how can he be useful in crying out as a *herald* of the word? If the watchman is not skilled in knowing the people, or living among them, to know them, how can he minister *to them* God's particular message? The word used here for "hear," links the watchman to the watched, who hear and obey the Lord's word, for God's glory and their good. It is linked not only to hearing, but hearing to obey the Lord. He does not have an office over the church to merely tell the people what they should do without doing it himself. He first hears the word, follows the word, obeys the word and can never expect any person to do anything that he is not willing to do. "For Ezra had prepared his heart to seek the law of the LORD, and to do it, and to teach in Israel statutes and judgments," (Ezra 7:10). You see, all these are set together in Ezra 7. The watchman is out for the glory of Christ, and will never tell them, "do as I say but not as I do." He is sensitive to the leading of the Spirit, and direction in bringing the Spirit's desire for the church at the time the Spirit desires it, that they might all walk abundantly in eternal life through God's Christ. If he is not praying and seeking the Spirit for spiritual persuasion in his study for those he watches over, or if he is not engaged in study, what will he know, and what will he say? He will either fill up his sermonizing with stories and, well, nothing of value, or he will try to wing it, which is equally abhorrent. God never tells the watchman to wing it as it concerns God's glory and Christ's dignity. God *always* tells the watchman exactly what to say. "Arise, go unto Nineveh, that great city, and preach unto it the preaching that I bid thee," (Jonah 3:2). To preach anything other than God's message in God's word for the glory of Christ, would be irresponsible and sin against the office, sin against the Christ, the church, the Spirit, and the Father. It does not bring God glory to do otherwise, and Christ will never be ministered in the church in those settings; he is not in *things* that are not his word.

As a consequence, such a watchman is skilled in preaching. For God tells him, "...and warn them from me," (Ezek. 33:7). He preaches to the people on behalf of God to show them the Christ. He is skilled to do it, and knows the content of the message he is to deliver. In looking at such a passage throughout, there are warnings, commands, promises, arguments, of both a practical and theological nature in Ezekiel 33. The watchman deals with people affected by the fall, and they must know how to deal faithfully in their skill of preaching well; communicating well to snatch that soul from the fire of hell. They must even show forth a growth in their preaching, to be better in their preaching as they preach. But regardless of how much better they become, they have the proper preaching skills to preach to the people on behalf of God; they are apt to teach: because the watchmen in this way is the Lord's voice. He is skilled in preaching, or literally, *to speak distinctly.* Does this not fit exactly what God has said about his watchmen? In doing so he deals with God for the people and deals with the people for and from God. This is accomplished by the word of God, the text itself, the letter of the voice of God. That is where God's glory lies. In preaching it is done by interpreting, expounding, and applying the word to the edification of the church; showing forth the text, its truth and its life application. He is a herald sent to proclaim to the world the Messiah, the one who redeems and saves by God's appointment and power. How does he do this? He does this boldly, faithfully and plainly. Boldly, as having authority, as representing the person of Messiah the Prince that sends him. Faithfully, neither adding to, nor detracting from what they have received in instruction from Christ in the word by the Spirit through serious study. Plainly, that everyone to whom they preach, may hear God's message openly and freely. God does not give this commission to just anyone. He chooses those right for the task and sends them on behalf of his word to bring warning and comfort to the people of the covenant.

And why is he skilled, but that, such a watchman is responsible before God for this ministry to them! They are responsible down to the very blood of the people destroyed, in this case, by judgment, if Christ is not proclaimed. They are responsible to cry out, to lead, to guide to demonstrate the Law of God,[5] the work of Christ, the salvation and Gospel that brings people into eternity having a mind to be responsible to God first. This is really why the watchman does not fear men, for the watchman fears God. He cannot be silent, and he cannot change God's message to make it more palatable. God says that the silent watchman is damnably guilty. Imagine the judgment, then, on those who try to silence their watchmen, or the watchmen who allow themselves to be silenced?

How will Christ be preached to the people if the watchman does not do it? What will be the outcome of

---

[5] See my work, *The Ten Commandments in the Life of the Christian* for a more complete study on the commandments.

bringing glory to the Father in such preaching and praying, and seeing the work of the Spirit applying Christ to the people in forgiving them and ministering Christ to their heart, soul and mind?

The watched must take heed to the word of the watchman, for that is where Christ is found. God who has ordained his watchman to watch, has also ordained the watched to hear that they might exercise faith in Jesus Christ, and find him. "Faith commeth by hearing, and hearing by the word of God," (Romans 10:17). Hearing, by the word of God, that is, by his watchman, in the ordinance of preaching. The watched must attend on it, because it is God's ordinance, and they are negligent if they do not. John Brinsley said, "There is a great deal of force and strength in this argument, to persuade men to attend on the hearing of the word preached, because it is God's own ordinance. A man may always expect to find God when he seeks Christ in God's own way. Then may a man comfortably assure himself of a blessing, when he seeks it in the ordinance of God, in that way which God himself has sketched out, and appointed for that end and purpose."[6]

God makes all things useful to the watched by his Spirit, because if God is glorified in the act of hearing and doing, it is where Christ is found. Do people want to find more of Christ? How will they drink deeply of him or suck virtue from him; how will they know Christ loves them? The watchman makes every comfort in

---

[6] Brinsley, *Preacher's Charge*, <u>Part 7: Hearing the Word Preached</u>.

Christ to be comfortable for those watched over for his glory in the word. It may be sometimes, that preaching is sharp and pointed, at other times, sweet and tasty. But all of it is God-glorifying if the watchman is bringing the Lord's voice to the city. He makes every means of their good to be helpful and serviceable to them, for God's glory.

Preaching is God's ordinance and there is a word of command that goes along with direction for the watched, to hear well. It is the watchman's charge to preach, and the people's charge to hear. These bring glory to God and Christ, and Christ is ministered among the people that they may be conformed into his image, and be turned *into him* more and more. In God's grand counsel and purpose, he has set apart the only ordinary means for the beginning, increasing, perfecting the work of grace in the hearts of his watched people, and so to be his power to salvation through watchmen in preaching. He has given the heralding of the watchmen for this very end and purpose, for the glory of his Christ who redeemed them, and forgives them.

There is a grand ministerial charge from our text. Be reminded that only God can make a watchman over his church, a minister of the Gospel, and the watched listen to those ministers that are of God. God alone is the author of all offices in the church and no one can take up the office unless God has sent him. To attempt any work in the office of the minister without his help, and without his blessing, without his commission, is to fail at the outset. As men are called into office, for a specific need in the church, it is a weighty matter, because they minister Jesus Christ to your soul. This is why Paul told Timothy, "Lay hands suddenly on no man," (1 Tim. 5:22), Paul instructs Timothy because of the nature of the criteria, not to be rash in ordaining men. In many churches, men are swept into the office of an elder to keep a family or a person in that church. To give them something to do; to make them feel important; "let's give them a ministry so they'll stay."

Ministers in the church, must think very differently about being a watchman, and about those they watch over, because they are the ordained means of bringing glory to God and exalting Christ in the midst of the people. And as a minister of the Gospel, a watchman for God, for the exaltation of Christ and the glory of God, for the good of the people, such men must recognize that they are set apart and called primarily to watch and pray; this brings God great glory; and within that scope, Christ will be ministered to the people. Does your minister, reader, watch and pray for you? Such watching and praying is culminated in the exercise of the word, in preaching and praying. Such is to be done for the glory of Christ, in knowledge of the word, preaching with boldness, faithfulness, and in clarity for your good.

God alone makes the watchman and sets him over his church to exercise himself in those two primary duties. This is something that, after ordination, cannot be eradicated or taken away. God makes a minister, and until the day they die, they preach God, the Christ and his Gospel, that *Our God Reigns* through the work of Christ crucified, that God may be glorified and the people forgiven and transformed into better Christians. For, "he gave some, apostles; and some, prophets; and some, evangelists; and some, pastors and teachers; For the perfecting of the saints, for the work of the ministry, for the edifying of the body of Christ:" (Eph. 4:11-12). This is why men must be called and qualified to that task for the good of your soul.

What doctor would you go to for surgery who was a "C" student? "Yes, I got a C on brain surgery, but I managed to get through it ... so when can we set an appointment for me to perform surgery on your brain?" Who would go to such a person? We don't tend to give into things that are *life and death* as it pertains to our physical bodies, but we tend to do it with things that are life and death *to the soul*, things that have eternal realities attached to them.

If a person desires the office, as a watchman, they are to preach on behalf of Christ and to pray to Christ on behalf of the people, to the glory of God. To preach on behalf of Christ and the Gospel of Christ, is the greatest work they can do in the world, because they have been called and commission to it. It might be as with Jeremiah they are compelled to do it, though it is hard. "Then I said, I will not make mention of him, nor speak any more in his name. But his word was in mine heart as a burning fire shut up in my bones, and I was weary with forbearing, and I could not stay," (Jer. 20:9). Such consists in four actions that they must take up to discharge the office faithfully, before God, responsibly, as a watchman over the flock, to glorify Christ.

[1] In demonstrating God's glory and will through Christ and his covenant, by demonstrating the truth of the word concerning the living word that brings eternal life. They preach the sweetness of Christ's character, person, natures, the Godhead, manhood, his offices, his covenant, his incarnation, birth, life, death, resurrection, ascension, intercession, exaltation and coming again at the last day. They are specifically commissioned and trained up for this. How will a man show another where his righteousness comes from but through God's Christ?

[2] In instructing that God will save sinners by Christ, and only by the Christ. God has set Christ as the only means of reconciliation; only through Christ may people come to God. They are to demonstrate the God they come to, and the means God has set down to obtain that end. "Turn and live," God says in Ezekiel 33 to sinners. It is the watchman's job to show men how this is done. And it is never done by the lackadaisical attitude of "Everything will work out fine in the end, just go with the flow."

[3] They preach the manner in which God has ordained sinners to come to Christ, and to God by the Christ, and this is by faith, (Rom. 10:8), and faith alone,

which is the only instrument ordained of God to take hold of the Savior, and to apply the merit of his active and passive obedience for eternal life. Faith comes by hearing, and hearing by the word which they preach. There is no other way.

[4] They apply Christ by commanding sinners in the name of God to believe in him, (Acts 16:31), to receive him as Savior, to have an interest in him, and to rest on him, and to repent of their sins before him; that they may be forgiven. The substance or boiling down of the ministerial office is in those four doctrinal walls which watchman must live and breathe in. They will also pray on behalf of the people to Christ. They are to give themselves habitually to effectual fervent prayer for the church of Christ in general, and especially for those of their particular charge in the church they minister in. "But we will give ourselves continually to prayer, and to the ministry of the word," (Acts 6:4). This is the very substance of the watchman. "Watch ye therefore, and pray always," (Luke 21:36). "Watch ye and pray, lest ye enter into temptation," (Mark 14:38). "Take ye heed, watch and pray: for ye know not when the time is," (Mark 13:33). All kinds of practical points emerge from this kind of watching and praying, taking heed in light of devotions before God and living before him; of the combat against sin; of the quality of abundant life in Christ daily; of coming judgment, all kinds of Christ-glorifying acts. They are to pray always for their people, specifically, and diligently, which means they must

know what their needs are and this in and of itself means they are familiar with their needs. "Then said I, Woe is me! for I am undone; because I am a man of unclean lips, and I dwell in the midst of a people of unclean lips," (Isa. 6:5). Paul prayed always for his people. "Wherefore also we pray always for you, that our God would count you worthy of this calling, and fulfil all the good pleasure of his goodness, and the work of faith with power," (2 Thess. 1:11). "Now I pray to God that ye do no evil," (2 Cor. 13:7). "And this I pray, that your love may abound," (Phil. 1:9).

As much as Scripture outlines all this, and more, I am also obliged to mention the charge of the office according to our confession as well. Charges are often solemn. "I charge thee therefore before God, and the Lord Jesus Christ, who shall judge the quick and the dead at his appearing and his kingdom; preach the word; be instant in season, out of season; reprove, rebuke, exhort with all longsuffering and doctrine," (2 Tim. 4:1-2). Why? "I travail in birth again until Christ be formed in you," (Gal. 4:19). Christ is to be formed in the people for the glory of God. What, then, must the watchman do, so that you can hear? So, I want to take a final remark of reminding you of certain parts to the *Westminster Confession* on ordination, as to what is expected of the watchman. How can a church glorify Christ in watching and being watched, if the watchman or the watched don't know what Scripture says about preaching and praying, or hearing and doing? I give this by way of summary, so that you see how Christ is ministered to the people by the watchman, and how the people are to think about what the watchman does in Christ's stead on earth, while the Lord tarries.

First, it belongs to the office to pray for and with the flock, as the mouth of the people to God (Acts 6:2-4, Acts 20:36). How many churches don't pray together? This is where preaching and prayer are joined as several parts of the same office, (James 5:15). The office of the watchman, the elder, that is, a pastor, is to pray for the sick, even in private, to which a blessing is especially promised: much more therefore, ought he to perform this in the public execution of his office, as a part of it, (1 Cor. 14:15-16).

That the watchman is to read the Scripture publicly (be reminded of Ezra); the proof of this shows that: 1. That the priests and Levites in the Jewish church were trusted with the public reading of the word, (Deut. 31:9-11; Neh. 8:1-2. 13). 2. That ministers and watchmen of the gospel have as ample a charge and commission to dispense the word as well as other ordinances, as the priests and Levites had under the law, proved, by Isa. 64:21; Matt. 23:34, where our Savior entitles the officers of the New Testament, (Matt. 28:18-20; Eph. 1:20-22, compared with 4:8-11, and Psalm 68:18) whom he will send forth, by the same names as the teachers of the Old Testament. That is why, for example, Hebrews uses the term *watchman* for pastors because they are the same in every age. This proves, that the duty of the watchman being of a moral nature follows by just consequence, that the public reading of the Scriptures belongs to the office. Simply, to feed the flock, "by preaching of the word, according to which the office bearers teach, convince, reprove, exhort and comfort, to bring glory to God through the ministry of Christ to the soul," (1 Tim. 3:2; 2 Tim. 3:16-17; Titus 1:9). This kind of view to preaching is very God-glorifying; it is the supremacy of God seen in preaching the Christ, preaching the word.

And then, how many churches have you been in where this has taken place: as the confession says, to catechize, which is a plain laying down the first principles of the oracles of God, (Heb. 5:12), or of the doctrine of Christ, and is a part of preaching? This is to dispense such divine mysteries, (1 Cor. 4:1-2), such as to administer the sacraments, (Matt, 28:19-20; Mark 16:15-16; 1 Cor. 11:23-25, compared with 10:16). To bless the people from God, Num. 6:23-26, compared with Rev. 14:5, (where the same blessings, and persons from whom they come, are expressly mentioned), Isa. 64:21, where, under the names of priests and Levites to be continued under the gospel, are meant evangelical pastors, who therefore are by office to bless the people, (Deut. 10:8; 2 Cor. 13:14; Eph. 1:2). As it is warranted, to take care of the poor, (Acts 11:30, 4:34-37; 6:2-4; 1 Cor. 16:1-4; Gal. 2:9-10). Working with deacons in the church for this end. And also, have a ruling power over the flock as a watchman, and under-Shepherd who has Christ as his Commander (preventative and corrective), (1 Tim. 5:17;

Acts 20:17-28; 1 Thess. 5:12; Heb. 13:7-17). The watchman is under authority to bring Christ to the people in this way. "By zeal and faithfulness, in accordance with the Spirit's power working in the minister, he is to maintain the truth of the gospel in all this, and unity of the church, against error and schism."

Consider, then, in all this, preaching and praying, and hearing and doing; of the greatness of the office and work, the danger of its negligence; the responsibility of the people; for watchman faithfully to discharge their office by directing to and exalting Jesus Christ first and foremost, which is the work of the Gospel ministry, and that the watched receive him in all his power for the glory of God; all those who do not do this, nor care to do this, are negligent watchman at best, and false shepherds at worst.

FINIS

Other Helpful Books Published by Puritan Publications

Consider some of Dr. McMahon's other works:

John 3:16, Second Edition
5 Marks of a Biblical Church
5 Marks of Biblical Commitment to the Visible Body of Christ
5 Marks of a Biblical Disciple
5 Marks of Biblical Reformation
5 Marks of Christian Resolve
5 Marks of Devotion to God
A Practical Guide to Primeval History
Augustine's Calvinism
Christ Commanding His Coronavirus to Covenant Breakers
Eternity Weighed in the Balance
Covenant Theology Made Easy
Historical Theology Made Easy
How to Live Every Day in the End Times
Joseph's Resolve and the Unreasonableness of Sinning Against God
Seeing Christ Clearly
Systematic Theology Made Easy
The Five Principles of the gospel
The Two Wills of God Made Easy
The Reformed Apprentice, a Workbook on Reformed Theology
The Reformation Made Easy

Also, consider these newly published puritan works:

A Call to Delaying Sinners
by Thomas Doolittle (1632–1707)

A Treatise of the Loves of Christ to His Spouse
by Samuel Bolton, D.D. (1606-1654)

Attending the Lord's Table
by Henry Tozer (1602-1650)

Faith, Election and the Believer's Assurance
by George Gifford (1547-1620)

God is Our Refuge and Our Strength
by George Gipps (n.d.)

Remembering Your Creator
by Matthew Mead (Mead) (1630-1699)

Resisting the Devil with a Steadfast Faith
by George Gifford (1547-1620)

Taking Hold of Eternal Life in Christ
by George Gifford (1547-1620)

The Believer's Marriage with Christ
by Michael Harrison (1640-1729)
The Blessed God

A Watchman Over Christ's Church

by Daniel Burgess (1645-1713)

The Doctrine of Man's Future Eternity
by John Jackson (1600-1648)

The Victorious Christian Soldier in Christ's Army
by Urian Oakes (1631–1681)

Zeal for God's House Quickened
by Oliver Bowles B.D. (1574-1664?)

www.ingramcontent.com/pod-product-compliance
Lightning Source LLC
Chambersburg PA
CBHW030849090426
42737CB00009B/1164